Walking in Circles

Walking in Circles

Essays

James M. Wright

Metamorphic Press

Copyright © 2023 by James M Wright

All rights reserved. No part of this book may be reproduced in any manner whatsoever without written permission except in the case of brief quotations embodied in critical articles and reviews.

First Printing, 2023

CONTENTS

DEDICATION — vii

1. Walking in Circles [Wales 2018] — 1
2. Within the Max Euwe Center [Amsterdam 2017] — 21
3. Grykes and Clints in the Karst [Inishmore 2018] — 29
4. The Poet's Well [Kilcrohane 2018] — 39
5. City Full of Dreams [Paris 2017-2018] — 46
6. The Coin Purse in Theory and Practice [Ennis 2018] — 85
7. The Stones We Leave Behind [Carnac 2017] — 88

CONTENTS

8 | Putting the Body Back Together
[Crete & Naxos 2019]   96

AFTERWORD   133
BIBLIOGRAPHY   135
ABOUT THE AUTHOR   137

For Susan, of course.

1

Walking in Circles [Wales 2018]

In a dérive one or more persons during a certain period drop their relations, their work and leisure activities, and all their other usual motives for movement and action, and let themselves be drawn by the attractions of the terrain and the encounters they find there.

Guy Debord, "Theory of the *Dérive*"

My wife and I love to walk. We walk everywhere we can: city, country, or wilderness. I like to have an objective, even if we don't get there. In the spirit of the *flâneur*, Susan prefers to have no destination at all. We've learned to tolerate each other's shortcomings. We walk side by side or single file, depending on the path. Often silent, we like to feel the inner stretch along our bones and the rhythmic impact of the earth underfoot. Sometimes we stop, stare at the surroundings, take a photo, chat about the rattling in our heads, or turn around and look back where we've been.

One of the best places to walk is the United Kingdom, where it's considered a respectable activity. The Brits, long accustomed to eccentricities, don't look twice when their countryside and villages are occupied by stick-wielding ramblers in khaki pants and floppy field hats. On the contrary, tramping around for the joy of it is accepted and encouraged, even by those who don't do it. As a result, there are systems of pedestrian pathways covering most of the landscape, linking marked trails, old farm lanes, and rural rights of way. Walkers drawn to the myriad of wandering byways need services, and in many economically distressed areas, providing these services has become a significant business. Some farmers complain about the unpredictable interactions between hikers and livestock, but many residents experience a renewed pride in their land when they see it through the eyes of ramblers awestruck at every stream, meadow, and overlook.

Welcoming the opportunity to go big, Wales established a continuous walking route along its periphery, a defining circle of the nation. The 840-mile Wales Coastal Path follows this natural boundary along a rugged seaside trail incorporating every available type of right-of-way. Some sections of this meander are notable for their stunning beauty; other sections simply steer the rambler through fields of sheep shit. Inland, the circle incorporates Offa's Dyke Path, named after the eighth-century Anglo-Saxon King who built the giant berm to keep the Welsh in their domain and out of his. The pathway on the dyke still marks the 177-mile border between Wales and England. Via coast and dyke, you can circumnavigate the entire country on foot, should you wish to walk a thousand miles.

We visited Wales in the spring of 2013 and hiked a hundred-mile section of the Coastal Path, following the ancient pilgrim's way along the shore of the Lleyn Peninsula. For pilgrims past and present, the goal is Bardsey Island, a bleak mound off the tip of the peninsula. They say twenty thousand saints are buried out there and possibly King Arthur, although he seems to be buried several other places as well. Starting on the north side at Castle Caernarfon, it took us a week to walk to Land's End, where we saw Bardsey across a strait of churning seas. The winds pounded us and drove out any temptation to visit the graves of saints or kings. Turning our backs on the holy, we took another week to return by foot on the south shore of the peninsula. On both sides of this narrow finger of land, with each step, we walked through a land of mythological echoes, sea cliffs, tumbledown castles flying the green and white dragon flag, stone chapels, endless green fields, sideways rain, and teenagers speaking Welsh like their own secret language.

Five years later, we returned to Wales. By then, age and injuries had forced us to reevaluate our commitment to through-hiking. There's a freedom in that form, but not if you can't tote the loads between lodgings. You can pay people to ferry your bags from one B&B to another, an option we refused to consider because it seemed like cheating. With that settled, this time we decided to explore the Isle of Anglesey on day walks from a single hub. We only had a week anyway and there was no possibility of circumnavigating the island in that time. We rented an isolated cottage near the western shore and figured there would be no shortage of walking, especially since we refused to lease a car (also cheating).

Anglesey's coastal path is a sub-circle to the grand round of Wales, like an eddy on the edge of a vortex. The trail covers 125 miles even though the island is barely fifteen in diameter. Most of the coastline is considered an "AONB," an acronym applied by bureaucrats to certain natural assets: Area of Outstanding Natural Beauty. I found no reason to quibble with the designation, although the trail itself is catholic and passes everything on the coast, including a Royal Air Force base for fighter jets, a golf course of biological monotony, and Anglesey Circuit, an auto racing track that publishes a daily "noise diary." These were a few things we found to be less than outstandingly beautiful. But humans are adept at filtering reality to suit our proclivities and we have a high tolerance for dissonance. A few profane interpolations hardly defined the landscape in an otherwise steady progression of cliffs, grand estuaries, wheeling sea birds, and adjacent expanses of greener grass and bluest water. Even the occasional caravan park suggested no more than a proletarian ambition to share the wonder of sea and sky.

The tourist bureau promotes the notion of "circular walks," and they've gone to the trouble of posting attractive signs at every point of access to these circuits. Walking on one circle sometimes brings you to a junction with another, suggesting a perpetual looping ramble that may or may not bring you back to your starting point. Perhaps the fascination with roundabouts derives from the island's circular geography. Walking around the whole thing is a laudable achievement, earning you not only bragging rights, but an official adventure patch, suitable for sewing onto your field hat or vest.

Circular walks evoke a communion with the old ways, echoing traditional rituals. At holy wells, pilgrims walk three times around the well, turning motion into prayer. Without a doubt, there is something tidy in the concept of a circular walk: no ground is covered twice. I appreciate the gestalt of circles, but that's hardly the end of geometry. The method of the *dérive* encourages an open approach to the world; exploration becomes creative action. When walking embodies freedom, the best routes escape structure and predetermination. My wife and I strive for both through a consensus of differences, embarking with a plan, but following it only until we get distracted. In the end, all that really matters is that we find our way home before dark.

Our first morning in the Anglesey cottage found us dawdling over breakfast. This was our usual approach. Susan enjoyed her coffee while I studied maps and guidebooks, pausing only to shovel in more cereal. We decided that this day we were in a linear mood, so we chose to walk south along the Coastal Path to see the Neolithic chamber of *Barclodiad-y-Gawres*. The guidebook translated the Welsh into even more torturous English as "Giantess's Apronful" with a reference to the "large number of stones which were undoubtedly part of the original mound." Reading on, I learned that a primordial goddess named Cailleach, a giant, had the habit of wandering the long-ago Celtic Isles toting rocks in her apron. As she lightened her load, the droppings formed barrow mounds. This legendary whimsy, along with the promise of a "magnificent setting" finally got us moving from the cottage before lunch.

As we made our way along the several miles of path to the chamber, I regaled Susan with everything I'd learned from my research. She walked ahead at a brisk pace. Supposedly, we would see upright stones carved with spirals and chevrons in the same style as Ireland's Newgrange monument. Nowhere else in Wales could this be found! I was stoked, but I'm not sure I convinced Susan of its importance.

The structure turned out to be both more and less than expected. The existing stones of the chamber had been originally covered by dirt and grass, customary for all barrow mounds in Western Europe. Unfortunately, erosion had carved away at the mound. Archaeologists excavated the site in the early 1950s. As soon as they finished, preservationists entombed the remains under the domed roof of a concrete bunker. In a demonstration of forward thinking, at some point the restorers also placed solar panels on the summit of the mound to power an interior lighting system, the better to inspect the complicated carvings. For the final touch of preservation, the inner chamber, where most of the engraved designs are found, was imprisoned behind a wall of steel bars. When we arrived at this intriguing antiquity, the cell door was locked. We clutched the bars and peered into the gloom, seeing nothing. We could only admire the view over the sea before walking back to our cottage.

Further research revealed that the key to the chamber was kept at the local market and for a deposit of ten quid, anyone could borrow it. We resolved to do just that, even though the village of Llanfaelog was a mile from the cottage, in the opposite direction. Getting there involved a precarious journey along the pavement shoulder with occasional leaps into the weeds to avoid unsympathetic motorists. We'd already figured out that hoofing back and forth to the market would be a daily experience, given that it offered the only source of food in the vicinity. Our first inspection of the shelves had left us gloomy about the coming week of meals. I noted an extensive selection of biscuits and packaged cakes. We also inventoried abundant bags of crisps, a cornucopia of jams to accompany the mushy white bread, potted meats of uncertain derivation, and, for a fresh vegetable, a bin of last year's potatoes. Hot bangers could be purchased at the counter. I don't even remember what we ate on Anglesey; I've blotted it out of my mind.

That afternoon while Susan scoured the market hoping to put together a healthy dinner, I asked the clerk about the key to the chamber of *Barclodiad-y-Gawres*. Eyebrows were raised and, after some fumbling under the counter, a ledger was found. Yes, it was right there, the key, but I could only have it for a short period of time, like an hour, and would have to return it directly in case someone else wanted it. I did the math. We would have to tramp into town the next morning, get the key, walk to the mound, see the inside, and walk straight back to the market. At our fastest walking pace, I estimated that we would fall short of the necessary time frame by at least a factor of four. However, I said nothing and accepted the conditions, promising that we'd stop by in the morning. I didn't want to raise complications that might decrease our chances of obtaining the key, because by this point the experience had moved into the realm of mythic tasks and I wasn't about to muck it up.

The next morning dawned cloudless and at the market I handed over a ten-pound note, scrawled my name in the ledger, and earned the key. Eagerly, we strode the four miles to the mound. Key met lock and we were in. I flicked the light switch on and off at least half a dozen times before concluding that the solar system didn't work. Luckily, I'd brought my headlamp. Together, Susan and I went from stone to stone, inspecting the complex geometric figures and beautiful, precise spirals. Indeed, I saw resemblance to the famous carvings of Newgrange, a subject I'd studied with passion. I felt vindicated that my research mania, for once, might not have been a waste of time.

When we were done with our inspection of the interior, we walked out into the sunshine and looked over the undulating Irish Sea as it slammed against the cliffs below. We perched on the apex of a grassy promontory, admiring the sea in motion; it was like being on the prow of a giant ship. No wonder Cailleach dropped her rocks on this spot, claiming it for the gods. Over the following days we kept seeing this defining point of land—visible for miles around—from different vantages on our walks, a focal point of orientation. I tingled when I recognized it from afar, acknowledging the hub of our revolving peregrinations. But of all the angles of view, the one from the shore to the north gave me chills. The green mound sat pretty enough above the cliffs, idyllic except for the entrance to the chamber, dead in the middle, a black maw to another world.

I wouldn't rule it out. The local culture is steeped in otherworld mythology. The medieval text of the Welsh *Mabinogion* identifies the town of Aberffraw (two miles down the coast past the chamber) as the location for the betrothal of Branwen, sister of Bran, legendary giant and king of Britain. The suitor was an ambitious Irish king, who led an entourage across the sea to propose the match. Branwen, it goes without saying, was the most beautiful woman in the world. Anyway, after they got back to Ireland, the marriage ended badly, and Branwen had to be rescued by her brother, at the cost of his life. The inconsolable Branwen died of a broken heart, not far from the nearby town of Holyhead, where there's a cairn reputed to be her grave. Meanwhile, Bran's head had been removed from his body at his own request. Unfazed by the severance, the head continued to live on for nine more years, participating in the conviviality of the court, at least as far as such things are possible for a giant disembodied head. One can imagine the remnants of the royal family toting the head to the mound of *Barclodiad-y-Gawres* to enjoy the fine views or perhaps to keep a lookout for further Irish fishing expeditions.

As we inhaled the sea air and meditated on time and mythology, we watched a short, stout man carefully ascend the hill from the beach. He had a full, untrimmed beard, long stringy hair, and he carried a fishing pole. We heard him breathing hard as he approached our position. He caught his breath, and we exchanged greetings. With the magnanimity of gods, we offered to let him use the key, but he declined, waving it off as inconsequential. After all we went through to see the contents of the chamber, I was taken aback. However, he had more pressing concerns, such as conversation. It might be more accurate to say that he was interested in having an audience, and we looked like ripe candidates. Ordinarily, this kind of behavior annoys me, but he had a friendly smile, and didn't seem in the least creepy. Anyway, we had nothing better to do than hurry back to the market with the key. We leaned against the stonework of the chamber entrance and listened. It turned out that he was an avid medieval history buff, and without a prompt he launched into a series of stories about making costumes to wear at the nearby castle for tourist shows and hosting fairs and workshops in the old ways with fellow enthusiasts from his club. It almost goes without saying that he belonged to a club; of course, there was a club.

Susan and I learned many details of medieval technology, such as how knights used goose fat to prevent their armor from rusting. He identified himself as an amateur blacksmith. Anticipating a lecture on the minutiae of sword-making, I changed the subject with a question about future projects. The fisherman informed us that his latest ambition was to be accepted into the cast of a projected BBC show. Filmed on Anglesey, it would portray ancient techniques of living off the land. He called it a documentary, but it sounded like a reality show of the survival genre. The opportunity was so alluring that he was willing to live without his wife and children for six weeks. We weren't clear if the separation was a good thing or a bad thing, perhaps a relative matter. This day, however, he was working on a different goal, a long-term personal project to fish every corner of the Anglesey coast. Sadly, he was having no luck on the rocks below *Barclodiad-y-Gawres* and was ready to move on to the next bit or he feared there would be no fish for dinner. After repeated hemming and hawing and reluctant mutters of "I'd better get going," he wandered south along the trail. We wished him well and headed off the other way.

By the time we got back to the market, the counter staff had changed shifts. The teenage boy at the register had no idea what I was talking about when I attempted to return the key. He re-enacted the original fumbling search for the ledger, a routine I found interesting since it was rather a large hardbound volume and contained sufficient pages to cover the next thousand years of key rentals. Eventually, he found it and with a puzzled expression, took the key from me and handed over the ten-pound note stuck in the ledger as a bookmark.

After two days of hiking up and down the coast, we decided we'd try one of the circular walks. We left the cottage at a respectable mid-morning hour and picked our way with care through the grass and dunes toward the beach. This area had been colonized by a vast rabbit warren. At every step, small, brown rabbits erupted from clusters of high grass, bolting toward one of the numerous holes leading into their underground sprawls. It was impossible to walk this trail without rabbits exploding in frenzy left and right. By varying our pace and acting nonchalant, we hoped to display our benign natures, but they could smell on us the taint of cooked meat, I'm sure.

As we strolled the long arc of beach, Susan looked for shells, hoping to find a scallop, the pilgrim's symbol, like she found on our walk around the Lleyn Peninsula. We saw none, but she filled her pockets with whelks and cockles instead, as well as the odd polished stone so smooth that it was irresistible. These would all become offerings to adorn the windowsills of the cottage.

Turning away from the sea, we followed the trail inland through heavy gorse. We crossed a road to arrive at a small fresh-water lake in the middle of pastures, stone walls, and the occasional hardwood copse. According to our map, the path meandered through farmland along the shore, encircling the lake in a bucolic loop. The fields were small, which meant that walls were frequent. Each one required passing through a stile or "kissing gate." Actual kissing is optional; the term refers to the light touch between the gate components when they swing to and fro. These cunning portals are tricky enough to stymie livestock as well as the untutored walker. More than once we paused and stared at the moving parts like idiots, wondering if we were any smarter than the imprisoned beasts.

Instead of the usual sheep, in one of the pastures we met donkeys. The farmers had stationed placards with head shots of the donkeys along with their names so that wayfarers might talk to them as friends, though we were cautioned to feed them nothing but carrots. We had no carrots and even though we used their names, our presence failed to sustain their interest. One of them, I can't remember who, paused its core activities of eating and shitting long enough to give us a blank look.

We marched around the lake in no time and popped out back on the road. Although we had completed an official Anglesey circle, rather than an epiphany, we shared disappointment over the brevity of our walk. So, we reversed direction and went halfway back along the path until we came to a junction with another trail. This one burrowed inland through dense hedgerows bordering farm lanes. Occasionally we came to a gap in the hedge and could peer at a house, a field, or a flock of bored sheep.

Perhaps an hour later we escaped the vegetation tunnels to find ourselves in the village, standing in front of the church of St. Maelog, not far from the market. This modest church is a beauty of old stone. It doesn't have the majesty of the great cathedrals, which I find unappealing, anyway, with their cold, relentless domination of the spirit. St. Maelog's is built on a human scale, crafted from black basalt rubble along lines of simple geometry. Inside, the woodwork exudes a welcome warmth. The tree of life, an ancient Celtic theme adopted by the early Christians, can be seen in carvings and paintings everywhere in the chapel. The finely sculpted benches, tables, and ornaments evoke the form and texture of trees, so much that the place feels like a sacred grove. Even the pastor's lectern rests on a stand of curved branches. In the corner I spied a menorah, a different vision of the tree, and another branch in the diverse forest of the church.

I am not religious and only erratically spiritual, but I admired the grounded, authentic spirit of St. Maelog's. The word "holy," plain-spoken, felt just right. Within the entry chamber were shelves of books, a circulating library for the flock. That alone would have impressed me, since I require many books to be bibles. I picked up a bilingual pamphlet titled *Y Cylch Celtaidd*, "The Celtic Circle." Perhaps you thought I was kidding about the proliferation of the circle thing, but in Wales they take their symbolism raw and in large servings. In this case, the pamphlet referred to a circle of ten churches in the area. The churches are scattered about, and I noticed on the map that no line can be drawn between them that forms a circle. The word represents one of its other meanings, designating a link between people around a center of commonality, in this case, a heritage. I stood in the vestibule and studied the pamphlet; Susan explored the nooks and details of the church. I learned that St. Maelog's was founded in the year 605 although the current church was built twelve hundred years later, in 1848. As an American of uncertain belonging, it's difficult to comprehend this kind of continuity through time. I have little orientation to ancestors or homeland

and even my nomadic inclination has no real tradition behind it. The thought crossed my mind that if I lived here, I would probably attend this church. Not to worship a god, but at least to share a place where people and trees mingle in reverence.

We emerged from the cool, dimly-lit church into a sun-bright yard of graves, most marked by slabs of black slate, many tipped or sunken—skewed by the passage of time. Several monuments were carved from stone to resemble wood, with details of incised bark and branch stubs. These logs of rock were used as retainers for the banked earth over the tombs or shaped in the form of crosses standing sentinel over the buried souls. The names on the graves were typically Welsh: Jones, Roberts, Williams, Davies and such. I spotted an Owen, followed by an Owens. Excited, I looked for more. Owens was my mother's maiden name, and that's pretty much all I have for a legacy to her past and my maternal roots. I stepped with care around the older graves, and I was joined by Susan, who always loves a good hunt. And we found them: multiple generations of Owens. I was touched by the notion that these could be my own ancestors. This place, that spoke directly to my heart, might be a source, a home.

We walked every day, eager for new places and paths. Our routes resembled jumbles of lines trying to find their circles since we often got distracted or took the long way around. Once we learned how, we waited by the road for the regional bus to start or complete longer circuits. When we'd first arrived in the main town, Holyhead, our initial interaction with local transport had not been promising. No one in the train terminal had the slightest idea that there was a functioning bus service on the island. We thought differently because we had a timetable but knowing how to access the damn vehicle seemed to be uncommon information. With desperation, we dragged our luggage around town, boiling in the June heat, hoping to find the bus stop before we missed the last run of the day. We accosted people on the street, which yielded a series of shaking heads and nothing more. Finally, a nurse walking to work, dressed in her uniform and nametag, after some thought, guessed that we might find it "down there," and she pointed along a street.

We arrived at the stop out of breath and within minutes I watched in astonishment as our bus rolled down the pavement and straight past us without slowing. I waved my arms like a wild man, which caught the driver's attention and he braked to a quick halt. He proved to be a kind, blue-eyed Welsh-speaking gentleman who had no problem educating us in the ways of rural transport. As anyone knows who has traveled, finding such people is more valuable than gold and I clung to every nugget of his wisdom. Buses didn't actually stop at the designated and signed stops, he said—you had to flag them down. It turned out that you could get on or off the bus anywhere on the regular route; it was all about making your intentions known. The driver knew exactly where we were going. In fact, he knew the name and location of our cottage and he readily agreed to let us off in front of the house. This was an unexpected boon and I felt gratitude and relief at not having to portage our bags any further.

The driver reminded me of my father, old-fashioned and polite, but full of questions, and I stood next to his seat so we could talk whenever we rode his bus. He seemed to like that we chose to ride the bus or walk. Mostly, tourists drove cars and his few passengers were local children or elders. He promised to tell the other driver to look out for us on his day off so that we would get back to Holyhead in time to catch the ferry when our stay was done. I loved this guy's patience with his riders, shifting back and forth between Welsh and English as needed, chatting with everyone, and never expressing the slightest hurry while people, no matter how infirm, maneuvered themselves and their shopping carts on and off. Somehow, though, his bus was always on time. At the end of our last ride with him, we shook hands in solemn ritual.

Using the bus system extended our range and allowed us to visit other churches in The Celtic Circle. We decided that we had to see the church of St. Cwyfan, also known as The Church in the Sea, so called because it occupies a rock outcrop along the coast, accessible at low tide but otherwise surrounded by the Irish Sea. This humble variant of Mont St. Michel is tucked away in a cove along the Coastal Path. We almost didn't find it. If it wasn't for the potential of a bus ride home from Aberffraw we probably would have given up and trudged back to the cottage, abandoning the circle for a line. I blame this circumstance on deviating from well-oiled habits. My usual practice is to purchase a detailed trail map as soon as we arrive in an area. Unfortunately, amongst the meat sticks, cookies, and crisps of the village market I had failed to discover any items of topographic intelligence. The only map I had was one I had brought to Wales: a blurry print-out from the internet. I admit to having a fetish about maps; I'm always keen to mine them for information and a bird's eye view of the world. Sometimes I want them when I don't always need them. In recognition of that, I'd thought to make do with less on this excursion. A sad and frustrating plight because British maps are the best in the world and provide astonishing details for the walker, including the precise outline of every stone wall and building. Such information can be handy when navigating the rural maze of fields, lanes, and intermittent signage. Now, I was forced to make do with substandard issue. However, the Anglesey Coastal Path seemed to be well posted, and really, how hard would it be to follow the coastline? Easy, of course, until the trail abruptly cut inland and merged into the labyrinth of farm ways. Then the signposts vanished, and we found ourselves standing on a paved road, looking left and right, hoping for a clue.

We turned right, in the direction of the shore, thinking that we would soon find the trail. Instead, we found ourselves standing on the periphery of the Anglesey Motor Racing Circuit. This obstacle was not marked on my free internet map, and I was shocked to find it intruding into the Area of Outstanding Natural Beauty. The day before, we had heard the wasp-like buzzing of race cars, as if carried a great distance on the wind. I wondered about it, but figured it lay many miles away, in another land. But here we were, dumbfounded, only a few yards from the glossy tarmac as stock cars roared past. I thought I was going mad. We climbed a grassy hillock to get our bearings. Spread out below was the work of the devil. Tightly banked asphalt, graded to precision, arced and curled through acres of green. At the end of the access road an expanse of earth overlooking the sea had been scraped and covered with gravel, enough parking for a small city. Metal sheds enclosed rows of clanging repair shops. Speed machines, luminescent with color, perched on trailers, and waited their chance to burn through the world's supply of petrol. Clearly, we were not on the Isle of Anglesey Coastal Path.

Dismayed, we fled, retracing our steps out of the compound and on to the road, marching with our heads down, ignoring the looks of motorists as they drove past, heading to the track. Back at the last junction with the Coastal Path we immediately spotted the sign that we had missed, hidden in an overgrown hedge. We still had time to walk to the church and catch the last bus out of Aberffraw, so we pushed on with a kind of grim determination.

Stretching our legs, we loped down a narrow, twisty lane, thankful for the hedgerows that shielded walkers from the motor circuit. I wanted nothing more to do with that place. We congratulated ourselves on our escape and tried to forget the humiliation of being a pedestrian amidst a casino of cars. Rounding a bend, a hilly peninsula blocked the banshee noise of racing, and we heard only the sound of waves and seabirds, as if the demonic track had been removed from the earth. In front of us, a cove opened to the sea. Just offshore, perhaps as an offering to the god of storms, a squat, stone-walled pedestal sat on ledge protruding from the waves. Perched on top like a crown was The Church in the Sea.

The church, a tiny chapel, dates from the 12th century and has somehow managed to cling to its foundation for nearly a thousand years, shored up, repaired, and still in use. The foundation is an oval platform covered with grass, elevated enough to avoid all but the worst storms. It's a lonely place, one step from the sea. Fortunately, the tide was out, so we walked over a causeway and up a flight of stone steps to the top of the platform. The door to the church was locked but there were outdoor benches at either end: one to look inland across the rich fields and the other to look outward, to dream and stare over the fallow sea. I tried both benches, but settled into the seaward side, letting my eyes roam across the swells. It didn't take long to drift into a trance. I barely remembered to check the encroaching tide, which rose in subtle measure.

Susan wandered off to take pictures while I let my anxieties drain into the ground under my feet. It was good to sit and do nothing. After a while, though, I started entertaining a fantasy that we could be caught by the tide and forced to spend the night huddled together on the doorstep of the church, cursing the god that brought us here. This perverse image amused me until I realized that I hadn't seen Susan for a while. I imagined the worst and feared that in her zeal for a camera angle she might have fallen off the rock wall. I walked over to the edge and called her name, but the wind whipped my voice away. I panicked and raced around the church; she was nowhere to be seen. It was as if she had vanished from the earth. I couldn't think of anything else to do so I walked around the church again and there she was. She'd wondered why I disappeared and had been looking for me. It didn't take long to figure out that we'd been on opposite sides of the church, walking circles in the same direction, at the same time.

Eventually we hiked to five of the ten churches in The Celtic Circle, approaching along lines and arcs, depending on whim, convenience, or constraint. Just before leaving Anglesey, we walked back to St. Maelog's lending library so I could donate the book I'd finished reading, *Seven Pillars of Wisdom* by T.E. Lawrence. When I reached the end of the book, I thought that I'd never read a better one. Rich and layered, like Wales itself. Lawrence, though English, was born in Wales and it seemed appropriate to leave the testament of his visionary life in the sanctuary of St. Maelog's. I strolled around the graveyard again and looked for more of what I now regarded as my people. Except for The Church in the Sea, all The Celtic Circle churches were encompassed by graves, and the only reason there weren't any at *St. Cwyfan's* was because the storms had washed them away. Everywhere there were headstones I found the name of "Owens," or more commonly, "Owen." There were even a few that reflected the Welsh economy for names: "Owen Owens." Seeing the iterations of this name never failed to evoke a deep satisfaction in my wandering bones, as if another circle was complete.

We left Anglesey in a calm frame of mind, happy to have seen the land and walked its paths. If you're open to it, it's a place where every step conjures a spirit of antiquity. The island earth has consumed ages of history and prehistory, but it still seems close to the surface. Yes, there are distractions that obscure the layers of time, like the fighter jets and race cars. I also felt the gloom and the gray emptiness of the towns, none of which can claim prosperity. The glories of Wales may have faded, yet the story of Wales grows new branches. The language survives, the flag is flown proudly, and visitors are welcomed with kindness. Please come, they seem to say, walk the rounds, visit the holy places, and perform the rites of renewal.

2

Within the Max Euwe Center
[Amsterdam 2017]

It wasn't that easy to get in. Over and over, we pushed the buzzer at the front entrance of a nondescript office building overlooking the Max Euwe Square in Amsterdam. I don't know what I expected, but I didn't expect no response at all. Doubtless we were at the wrong place, but Susan disagreed, perhaps swayed by the enormous chess set in the plaza with pieces that required two hands to pick up and move, surely a sign of something. We peered through the glass into an empty hall that led to a flight of stairs. I couldn't imagine the interior contained a museum, especially one celebrating a national hero, the former chess champion of the world. Finally, a couple of guys sauntered downstairs and out the door, ignoring us, and we scooted in. We climbed to the second floor and walked down a long, low-ceiling hall ending at a wooden door with a simple placard proclaiming, "Max Euwe

Centrum." As soon as we stepped inside, an elderly man hobbled up to us and barred any further progress.

"You are here to see the machines?" he asked in heavily accented English.

I dodged the question. "We would like to see the museum."

"Ah, yes. I can give you a guided tour; takes twenty minutes." We were pretty sure we did not want the guided tour and I wanted to say so without hurting his feelings. He seemed kind, if overbearing, and I had no desire to be rude. But he paid no attention to my muttering and herded us into an alcove where he opened a small locker and said we would have to put everything in there. I stuffed in my backpack, and my coat, as well as Susan's coat. "You must also place your hats inside." Susan protested the loss of her hat, claiming that her hair was messy. He waved off her concern. "It is for your safety." Susan and I exchanged looks but it was obvious these demands were not negotiable.

After we were stripped of our belongings, he resumed his offer of a guided tour, which he reminded would take about twenty minutes. By this point I figured that he was daft, and the idea of a tour still did not appeal to me, comprising, as I was sure it would, the endless tangential ruminations so loved by docents everywhere. I said that we would like to browse. Disapproval radiated from his long face, but he reluctantly agreed to let us browse. He pointed out the location of the exhibit, directly across the hall and about six feet from where we stood. He wanted us to understand that it was arranged in a sequence, starting here. He also offered us coffee or tea. We made noncommittal noises, and he repeated the beverage offer in a way that suggested it wasn't entirely optional. Susan gracefully accepted the promise of a coffee while she ran to the bathroom to fix her hair. While our minder went for the coffee, I started browsing the glass cases of the exhibit. When he returned, Susan in tow, he informed me that I was going the wrong way and it started over there where he'd wanted us to start. He then handed me a written guide in English, which I accepted. I held the yellowed sheaf of stapled, 8 ½ x 11 sheets, twenty pages of actual typescript. The corners were bent and nicked, handled by decades of enthusiasts. It looked like the kind of homework your dog would eat, but without it I wouldn't have understood the labels on the displays, which were all in Dutch, of course.

The exhibit outlined the career of Max Euwe, chess champion from 1935 to 1937, still the only Dutch player to attain the championship. Not only that, but he won the title in a stunning upset, beating the formidable Russian, Alexander Alekhine, one of the great players in the history of the game. Euwe only held the championship for two years, but he lived a long and honorable life, which is more than can be said about Alekhine, who died at the age of 53 while choking on a piece of meat. An alternate theory proposed that he was assassinated by Soviet agents since Alekhine renounced his citizenship and played for France instead of Mother Russia. Either way, the circumstances were mysterious and have never been verified.

After Euwe's death, his wife endowed the Center as a memorial; when the endowment ran out, the city picked up the funding, although the indifferent presentation suggests that it's not a high priority these days. I guessed that the museum didn't see a lot of traffic, perhaps the occasional school field trip when someone remembered that once there was a famous Dutchman.

Currently, the center functions mostly as a resource center for serious chess players, and there are more than a few in this serious country. A library of over ten thousand chess books sprawls around the common room along with an assortment of tables where students can play through the games of the past, analyzing and debating variations, looking for an edge to enhance their own tactics.

The exhibit itself consisted primarily of articles clipped from newspapers and journals along with accompanying photographs from Euwe's scrapbooks. Mounted in a series of clear plastic cases, you could follow the media artifacts of his life from youth to death. I identified the photographs as belonging to one or the other of two types: group portraits of rumpled chess players assembled in front of hotels and other venues used as tournament sites, or opponents crouched over chessboards, heads in hands, lost in the struggle. Typically, it was the same men in the photos, year after year: mustachioed, bespectacled, myopic, and looking uncomfortable in their coats and ties. The ranks of grandmaster chess players were, and remain, a thin crowd. These are exalted heights, not easily reached.

Despite our stated preference for browsing, the guide kept appearing over our shoulders, launching into informational monologues. These lasted for several minutes and promised to unfold into variations that would make 20 minutes seem a mercy. Exasperated, I inserted a sophisticated question, just to interrupt the flow.

"You know about chess?" he asked in an incredulous tone. Lurking behind his query I discerned the supposition that visitors appeared mostly by accident, deviants separated from their tour of Amsterdam's highlights such as the red-light district; having crossed one too many canals, they got lost and wandered up to the second floor of an unmarked office building where they hoped for a blow job or a drag on some weed. Before I could answer his question, he said, firmly and with precision, "When you are done with the exhibit, I will show you the machines." After this pronouncement, he retreated behind a shelf of books on the other side of the center.

I don't know why I was so resistant to "the machines." He could have meant computers, which now rule the chess world and don't really interest me, or he could have meant antique automatons, creations that I find fascinating. Regardless, his insistent commands from the start of our visit catalyzed within me an adolescent opposition. I didn't dare ask about the machines; a simple question on my part ran the risk of exposing too many vulnerabilities for him to take advantage. After all, we were in a game of sorts, full of gambits and feints, maneuvers of social nuance, interactions of control. I knew the rules, and I wanted to win. As did he, I'm sure. Perhaps chess players are always playing chess.

Distractions aside, Max Euwe and his artifacts intrigued me. I knew of his contributions to chess theory from my own study of the game, but I knew nothing about his life. Thanks to the raggedy little handout, I learned that despite the nobility of his deeds, he remained a humble man. He seemed like a nice guy, somebody worth knowing. He praised Alekhine, his nemesis, as "a poet who creates a work of art out of something that would hardly inspire another man to send home a picture postcard." In contrast, the arrogant Alekhine was so furious at losing to Euwe in 1935 that he swore off drinking and smoking, blaming his defeat on intemperance. Rather than honoring Euwe's victory, he snarled that "There are some moves of mine in the first Euwe match which I actually simply cannot understand."

In the 1937 rematch, a sober Alekhine destroyed Euwe and never played another championship bout, taking the title to his death nine years later. Euwe, though dedicated to chess, was less obsessive. He taught physics and math in an Amsterdam high school for girls. There is a wonderful photo in the exhibit of Euwe surrounded by his students after he won the championship in 1935. Jumping and cheering, they express genuine exuberance, and Euwe's smile is like the sun itself. When the Nazis occupied Holland, Euwe quit teaching to become a grocer, supplying food to the resistance and hiding Jews. After the war he returned to teaching and played competitive chess through the early 50s, finally retiring to lead the World Chess Federation. He died respected and loved, a true hero. Alekhine cut a deal with the Nazis and spent the war playing chess in regions controlled by the Axis powers. Two vile, antisemitic articles appeared under his name in chess journals during those years. He repudiated authorship after the war, but evidence suggests that he wrote them. Like much else about his controversial life, he remains enigmatic.

I wandered back to the common room where Susan stood in the corner, coffee in hand, chatting with a younger man who spoke good English and seemed completely sane. He asked me if I still played, and we talked about the popularity of chess in the US. I sketched out a theory that chess would do better in the States if it could be made telegenic. He doubted my thesis.

I pointed out that boring games such as poker and billiards had somehow found a niche on television. My proposal was to televise speed chess. Games last a maximum of ten minutes and are not subtle. The addition of a sarcastic color commentator and a smartly clad female assistant to refill coffee cups and point to the big board would make it a sure thing. Perhaps his English was not good enough to grasp the plan since he remained skeptical even in the face of these failure-proof details.

I probably overstated the case. He smiled anyway and directed me to a small room containing hundreds of used chess books for sale. Used books are a weakness of mine and I abandoned our discourse to paw through the offerings. It didn't take long to find half a dozen volumes I did not need but certainly wanted. Recognizing that there would be no room in my travel bag for more books, I narrowed the selection down to one: *My Best Games of Chess 1924-1937* by Alexander Alekhine. This volume included selected games from both of his championship matches with Euwe. Of course, he only selected games that he won; you'd have to go to Euwe's books to see the other side. I picked the book not only for the sneering move-by-move commentary but because it was a first edition, published in 1939. A well-seasoned book, it felt comfortable to hold. Worth having, anyway, since Alekhine, even though a scoundrel, was a killer chess player. No doubt, I could learn something.

On the way out, our officious guide materialized and urged us to consider adding to the donation box, which he claimed was critical for continued operation of the Center. He said that they almost had to close it last year due to a lack of funds. I emptied all my remaining euros into the box. Money well spent, and I said so, because this was a place like no other. He agreed, noting that they had received visits from Kasparov, Kramnik, and other world champions, right where we were standing. Before he launched into further lists or offers to see the machines, we retrieved our belongings and edged out. Walking into the sunshine on the plaza, Susan was happy to have her hat back on her head, but I found myself carrying some regret. I should have let the obstinate fool show us the damn machines.

3

Grykes and Clints in the Karst [Inishmore 2018]

It is not clear who makes and who is made in the relation between human and machine.

Donna Haraway, *A Cyborg Manifesto*

With our bags jammed between our legs, Susan and I rode a crowded bus from Galway to Rossaveel, the ferry terminus for the Aran Islands. Another hour on the boat brought us, along with two hundred other tourists, to a concrete dock on Inishmore, the largest of the three islands. We trudged through the dispersing crowd, ignoring the line of guides soliciting passengers for a motorized tour of the island. The vehicles were mostly open buggies and small vans; some of them resembled hayrides. Tourists who didn't select a guided excursion rented bicycles;

hundreds were available. The remaining pedestrians wandered into the village, heading for the pub, the souvenir shop, or the sweater boutique. Excitement bubbled into the air as the passengers, freed from the confining boat, burst forth to mingle with the Irish and their remarkable landscape.

We paused in the village to consult the map. Our hostess lived about two kilometers out of town; she'd suggested it would be a pleasant walk. I cinched the waistband of my backpack and leaned into the burden while Susan rattled alongside, tugging her wheelie bag over the cracks and cobbles of the road. It was a sunny, warm day in June and the walking was lovely, especially after all the bicyclers and tour vans passed us and we had the one-lane road to ourselves. Soon enough, the sun did its work, and the transportation of our baggage became a labor of sweat. We might have considered a discouraging word. But the beauty of the island was irresistible and soon enough we found our hostess and her home overlooking the ocean. She put us in a tidy apartment at the top of the house from where we could feel the sea breeze and hear the joyful sounds of her daughter practicing the traditional flute.

Inishmore is a nine-mile-long narrow mound of stark limestone wedged into the Atlantic. There can't be more than a hundred trees on the whole island. The southern, wilder half contains an upland plateau of bare rock, tufted with outposts of wildflowers, grass, and weeds clinging to a low-lying existence. On the north side, overlooking the meager protection of Galway Bay, generations of dedicated soil-building produced pastures tucked between stone walls. Outside of the few human-built structures, nothing ventures far above ground level. It's not hard to imagine the fury of the oceanic storms that pound the island, raking it clean. The sky and the sea define this land and there's little respite from either.

On the second day of our week, we walked on sharp-stoned paths across the island to view the ocean from the cliffs; the wind burned our faces as we stared at the horizon's arc. A hundred feet below our stance, the land met the sea in a collision of overhanging rock and thunderous waves. On most days, the rain pours down, draining the surface of the island into its lithic core, ceding particles and fragments to the flow. Geologists use the term karst, a term for regions of water-sculpted limestone. The Inishmore karst is monochromatic. Except for interpolations of brilliant green vegetation, the island is dark gray, a swollen slab of rock that looks like a giant whale plowing the sea.

When rainwater runs across the limestone, it cuts the pavement in parallel grooves. Every storm, these gutters carry away a little more stone, carving out planes of rock which resemble sidewalks. Alternating fissures and planes look like the layout for a vast gridwork. In geology, the planes are "clints" and the fissures are "grykes", terms that clack with rocky percussion. As the rain cuts deeper into the stone, the grykes sluice away dissolved sediments. Undercut in time, the clints exfoliate into slabs which, for many years, supplied the mainland with tombstones. Large or small, sometimes the slabs are loose underfoot and resonate with a hollow clunk when stepped on, a surprise for the walker every time. These rectilinear fragments, a perfect building material, come in all sizes. If you wanted to construct something of stone, such as a wall, you could start anywhere on the island and the raw material would be at your feet.

Grykes get wider as they age under the rain. Many are filled to bursting with clumps of hardy flora, mostly green but speckled with wild color. Traversing a field from clint to clint, we admired these pioneers as we stepped over them. These are fields in name only, defined by centuries of wall-building, delineating the bedrock of the karst into a geometry of enclosures, often following the right angled gryke-lines, dividing and subdividing the island with the conceit of property. The contents of these enclosures may include a cow or two as anomalies on the sheets of stone. They nibble down the tufts until cycled to the next field. Gardens are rare. The walls themselves are truly Aran's natural crop. They defy common masonry conventions, with stones set vertically and askew as well as horizontally. Gaps and triangular holes left by the eccentric joints create the appearance of complicated lace work. Each wall presents a web of delicate balance resisting time and gravity. The entire island is fenced in this manner, divided into a myriad of fields, no two exactly alike, a thousand miles of stone walls.

On our third day we hiked along the old rocky road from the harbor of Kilronan. We followed this track up a steep grade and over the island's spine onto the plateau that stretches to the south shore cliffs. Where the road petered out, a hundred meters from the precipice, we came to a stone bench with an expansive view of the ocean. A plaque announced that the bench was "Dedicated to the memory of Brendan Gill, lost at sea." Off to the side, we noticed a walker's way sign stuck in a pile of rocks; tilted, it pointed vaguely across the karst in the direction of our objective: *Dun Duchathair*, an Iron Age Celtic structure known as the Black Fort.

The sky lacked a single cloud, leaving the sun in command, rare enough in these parts, and we were tired and thirsty, having already walked six kilometers. We would have liked nothing better than to sit on the bench and take in the view. However, a young woman occupied the space, hunched over the rectangle of her smartphone. I walked within a polite distance and offered a cheery hello. She didn't look up or reply. Apparently, her world didn't extend beyond the bounds of her digital slab. We wandered around her periphery, hoping that she would take the hint and yield the dead man's seat. She did not, and we settled for stepping over the wall that separated the bench from the last bit to the cliff edge, walked a few steps, and settled down on a smooth surface. Ordinarily, I wouldn't intrude into someone's view, especially in such a lonely place, but it seemed obvious that her eyes were lost in a private sea. My irritation vanished with the first bite of an orange, a juicy counterpoint to the sun and stone. As we gazed from our high platform over the rolling swells, Susan and I agreed that we had no desire to approach any closer to the frightening cliffs and their forty-meter vertical descent to the Atlantic.

While we ate our lunch, another young woman appeared on the road as if sprung from the bedrock. Without looking at the bench sitter or us, she marched with purpose straight to the brink of the cliff. Pulling a phone out of her pocket, she began to take selfies. It was terrifying to watch; a fear roiled out of my gut that she would create the perfect shot, post it to the world, and, with nothing left to achieve in life, dive over the edge in front of us. After several more minutes of modeling her trim figure, she spun and walked back to where we sat. Ignoring my smile, she zeroed in on Susan and without even a greeting, asked if she would take her picture. Never mind that Susan was mid-bite in mid-sandwich. Being a good sort, Susan set her sandwich aside and stood to take the photo. Rather than posing, the woman trotted back to the precipice, waving at Susan to follow. I doubted the wisdom of this venture, though it happened so quickly that I offered no objection. I should have said, "No fucking way, bitch, that's my wife!" Instead of that, while Susan followed, I fretted, sure that the woman either wanted Susan to document her suicide or, even worse, she wanted to take someone with her. Tense and incredulous, I watched as the woman demanded shot after shot of poses on the verge. Sensible Susan kept her distance. I couldn't wait until this scenario came to an end, but it did, without incident, thank god. Satisfied with her achievement, the woman turned and stalked off down the path back to the village, finished with her fifteen minutes at the view for which Brendan Gill gave his life.

Lunch completed, we abandoned the smartphone set and hiked away from the end of the road toward the Black Fort. We stumbled a lot as we negotiated the ninety-degree angles of the karst—left, right, straight, right, left, straight, and so on, not to mention up and down over walls and elevated clints. It was like one of those step-training workouts. There was no formal trail to the fort, but faint paths in the grass remained from the wanderings of other pedestrians. They turned here and there before fading into the rock. I found it easier to ignore the paths and navigate by clints, linking one to another, enjoying the throaty clunks resounding under our passage. We had to keep a careful eye on our feet to avoid the rim of the cliff. Erosion makes startling inroads into the island, cleaving away vast sections of stone, leaving overhangs and jagged edges, and sometimes blowing holes right through the rock from underneath. Even though we were twenty meters from the rim, at one point I looked down through a foot-sized orifice straight to the churning water. After that, we swerved further inland. If you can avoid pitching over the edge, you won't get lost in this stretch of the karst; the Black Fort dominates the landscape, a massive structure perched on the promontory. It's not hard to find; you just need to watch your step.

On the inland side, the fort presents a curved wall of dry-laid stones twenty feet high and eighteen feet thick, sealing off the tip of a cliff-bound peninsula. We roamed around the outside of the structure and marveled at the stonework that appeared as unmovable as a mountain. Against the lighter colored background of the sea, the fort looks black and sinister. It was easy to believe that we had walked out of our world into another place and time. The location is dream-like, and as the air shimmered between the sun and the stone, we felt the presence of myth, fantasy, and forgotten realms. At one end of the wall, we found enough space to allow passage into the fort. It was a narrow squeeze between the wall and the edge of a vertiginous drop into the ocean. After crossing, we agreed that looking down, though unavoidable, was a bad idea.

The interior of the fort contains a gentle swale of grass that barely covers the bedrock. The remains of several stone huts, called *clochain*, cluster near the main wall. Old steps led onto the ramparts, where you can look down over the remnants, out to sea, or inland across the stony landscape. I wondered what it would be like to huddle in this fortress with the livestock, walled into a precipitous cul-de-sac, theoretically secure against that ancient Irish tradition: the cattle raid.

I tried to imagine the old times, but I could not. As soon as we'd turned the inner corner of the wall, we encountered three scantily clad tourists laying on the grass. Two bronze women and a hairy man, all fit and shiny with body oil. Sun worshippers, it seemed, as they were sluggish, baked into torpor. One of the women raised up onto her elbow and said hello as we passed through her aura. We smiled and hurried across the fort and scrambled to the safety of the ramparts. We wanted to ignore them so we could daydream about the setting, but we were still distracted from the previous interactions and found ourselves, despite the amazing spectacle of the location, unable to disengage from the human race. I harbored some paranoia about the weird things that could happen way out here on the edge of the world. Unlike everyone else, we didn't have smartphones and couldn't call for help or search the internet for useful information or even send a final text to loved ones. Instead of letting ourselves drift into a trance and travel back in time, we spied on our fellow tourists and invented stories about who they were and what they were doing here. At one point they dragged themselves upright and paraded over to the wall where they took turns doing yoga headstands propped against the two-thousand-year-old stonework.

We noticed another woman wandering around the edge of the cliff. We were pretty sure she belonged to the same sect by the way she froze into yoga postures here and there, all close enough to the precipice to arouse my anxiety. Of course, she took selfie after selfie, no doubt seeking the perfect exposure. Susan mused that this is the new woman, glamorous and without fear, even on the brink.

We baked in the afternoon sun and studied the antics of the four bohemians. They huddled together at times but were too far away to overhear. After the edge-walking woman rejoined the group, I saw them pass a phone around like cultists with the sacrament. For a while, we tried to wish them away, like we did the occupant of Brendan Gill's bench, but it didn't work here, either. Like it or not, we had to share the Black Fort, Inishmore, and for that matter, the whole planet with people who didn't see it our way. Faced with the reality of our time, we put aside our scorn and laughed. Snickered, really, with our hands over our mouths. We didn't want to look rude. I learned long ago not to agitate strange characters, especially when you're outnumbered. Sure, they appeared harmless enough, just another entourage of tech-savvy pagans seeking rituals of spontaneous authenticity. It wouldn't have surprised me if they started fucking, but perhaps they had dispatched that duty before we arrived. At any rate, it was clear that their idea of reverence for place diverged from our own.

Tired of watching tourists under the sun and certainly tired of my grumbling philosophy, Susan suggested that we head back to our apartment. Giving up any hope for fantasizing about the Iron Age, I agreed. Perhaps we could stop in the village for ice cream, a commodity more representative of technological advance, in my opinion, than gizmos in your pocket. We scurried past the sunbathers, nodding with enough congeniality to avoid disrespect, but narrowing any openings for interaction. They were probably good people. Or maybe not, but we had no interest in settling the question.

Mystery and wonder rise from the rock of Inishmore in quantities sufficient to captivate the soul, yet in our day of wandering around the karst, everyone we encountered had eyes mostly for themselves. I don't know why I care about this so much; the earth doesn't. My own investment varies. I guess that's the human dialectic: some days we're like gods and other days, yes, something a lot more profane. Philosopher Paul Shepard commented that our machines are mirrors, and we saw plenty of that. Smartphones in hand as both mirror and lens, we peer at the world and our place in it. We can't stop fondling these tiny slabs made from heavy metals torn out of the earth and assembled by wage slaves. In a sense, we've traded our reliance on bedrock for a cyborg convenience. Will our attention to the future, ever so liquid in the best of times, drain away in digital grykes, leaving only silver slabs for headstones?

4

The Poet's Well [Kilcrohane 2018]

{For John Brogan, beloved teacher.}

...a [bardic] satirist was dissatisfied with the food given to him in the house of a certain nobleman. "Shall salt be sprinkled on your food?" said the servant. "No," said he, "for there is nothing to sprinkle it on, unless it be sprinkled on my tongue, and that isn't necessary; it is bitter enough already."

Eleanor Knott, *Irish Classical Poetry*

I noticed it on the map and wanted to go there, but it proved elusive. I'm talking about the Poet's Well, one of many archaic wells scattered throughout the Irish countryside. With a dot and the simple title "Holy Well," the charts reveal a land freckled with reservoirs of the sacred. This particular dot, halfway along the narrow Sheep's Head Peninsula of West Cork, wore a label less holy than lyrical, a powerful magnet for folks with literary inclinations, like Susan and me. Fulfilling my duty as navigator, I identified several rambles that would take us near the site. It seemed easy enough on paper; however, we soon discovered that when signs and markers in the earth are not provided, you're on your own in the wild mire of Ireland.

    It took us three times, which seemed right for the land of triads and trinities. The first time we took a wrong turn at a junction of paths and because the way ahead offered a path of such green perfection, we ended up walking it to the next town, telling ourselves that we'd see the Poet's Well another day. The second time, we tried to sneak in a walk between persistent rain squalls. We sloshed through wet grass along an exposed ridge and descended a path toward the location of the well, but the drizzle transformed into a dense sideways mist resembling a car wash. With slicker hoods up and heads down, we stepped right over the well without even recognizing it. Besides, our thoughts were too profane for holy matters, focused as they were on getting back to our cottage and getting out of the damn rain.

    The third time we used a methodical approach. The turbulent, unpredictable weather continued through the week, but on our last day it lifted enough to take a chance. Our method, difficult to define, started by walking down to the rocky beach of the bay where we wandered apart, lost in trance, evaluating the variety of driftwood, shells and seaweed tossed around the shore. My attention gravitated to the colors and shapes of the rocks. I kept picking them up and putting them in my pocket because they were special, then, after a while, discarding one or another because it was impossible to carry all the worthy rocks away from the beach. We reunited at the far end where giant slabs of stone bridged a stream. It was a good place to sit and compare our finds. We arranged them in rows along the bridge, admiring our choices. Susan noted that beach treasures appear remarkable at first sight but ordinary after a time, so we agreed to keep one each and leave the rest.

We climbed the path onto a grassy headland. There, tucked among the rocks under the crest of the hill, we found the crumbling remains of an ancient school. On some maps, this location is labelled "O'Daly's Bardic Seminary" because it was associated with the renowned O'Daly family, bards to the MacCarthy clan, longtime kings in medieval Munster. The bardic tradition in Ireland is so old that no one knows when it started, but traces survive from pagan times to the present.

The bardic school was a ruin of thick stone walls outlining the chambers where poets lived and trained. Any traces of roof had vanished, and the remains lay open to the sky, while vines and brush slowly pulled the stones back into the earth. I climbed up on top of the wall and gazed across the spectacle of Dunmanus Bay, a lovely sight and reason enough for the location of the school. It was easy to imagine dwelling in this place, until my contemplations fell on the modest chambers below my stance. They were barely large enough for a bunk or a pallet. Yet there the bards reclined in utter darkness all through the night, crafting poems in the mind, memorizing every word and phrase so it fit perfectly with the complex, rigorous forms of composition. Seven years of this kind of study and practice were required before a novice could take his or her place in society as a full-fledged bard.

Bards worked for patrons, who supported them in exchange for praise poems extolling the deeds and noble character of the benefactors. Part of the job also involved creating satires, vicious lampoons aimed at the enemies of the patron, or anyone, really, who annoyed the bard. The most famous O'Daly bard, Aongus Ó Dálaigh, composed so many satires that he finally met his end when an aggrieved subject took offense at a cutting verse and stabbed him to death.

From there we walked down the far slope of the headland and up the hill toward the mapped location of the Poet's Well. Legend has it that Aongus Ó Dálaigh stopped regularly to lap up its water for inspiration. Like the other holy wells of Ireland, this one continues to receive the visits of pilgrims, including local members of the ancient families. This time we approached with caution, ruling out rock piles along the way. Every boulder and outcrop was a candidate. *Is this it? No, let's go on.* Around a bend and there it was, unmistakable. Baffling that we'd missed it before; we had literally stepped across it to walk the trail. But, true enough, then it had just been another wet, muddy spot in a wet and muddy land. Today, as the sun pried through the rising mist, the well gleamed at us. At the base of a pale boulder was a neat, square pool of spring water rimmed with stones set into the ground, forming a basin about two feet deep. Next to the pool a modern coin sat on a flat rock, an offering left by another seeker. We looked at the well and looked at each other, then took out our treasures, placing them alongside the coin: a quartz-veined beach stone and a perfect scallop shell. Parting with them seemed much harder than parting with money; they were, after all, precious and irreplaceable. We then walked clockwise around the well. I thought about tasting the water, but the presence of green algae floating on the surface made me shy. I settled for anointing the tip of my nose.

Satisfied with our explorations and not wanting to press our luck with the weather, we walked back to the village and considered our options for lunch. As it turned out in this sleepy hamlet, there was one option: a pub that suggested many items on their outdoor menu with the disclaimer "depending on availability." We entered the deserted pub to meet Mary, who informed us that the only thing available was a toasted cheese sandwich. We chose the toasted cheese sandwich, then trooped outside to avoid the blaring television. Next to the road two picnic tables featured a prime view of town doings. The entire time we sat there, eating sandwiches and chatting, two cars drove past. A busy day.

After she delivered our sandwiches, Mary sat next to us, and talked at a ferocious pace. She informed us that she would never live here in Kilcrohane because of the bustle and noise; she preferred her isolated home on the other side of the peninsula. We also learned about the troubles of running an inn, especially the washing, which was endless and difficult to dry in the climate. She extolled the virtues of her fish dinners, regaling us with exotic menus that were currently unavailable. She worked her way up to the crowning moment of her presentation, an anecdote about two women tourists who insisted on adequate nourishment before setting out on their day hike. They ordered bowls of porridge, followed by the full Irish breakfast. Mary used her hands to demonstrate the size of the porridge bowls, certainly ample enough to feed a hog. She then recited each element of the full breakfast. It's an interesting concept, this breakfast, which turns out to be the same as the full Welsh breakfast and the full English breakfast. This typically consists of two eggs, ham, a slab of bacon, potatoes, peas, a mound of mushrooms, tomatoes, and miles of toast. It seems a suitable morning meal for farmers, day laborers, and others who have no need to tally cholesterol or carbohydrates. By any reckoning, it's a formidable serving. Mary was keen to convince us, though we were already well convinced, having previous knowledge of the meal, that the full breakfast following a bucket of porridge was undoubtedly excessive. And yes, she tried to talk them out of it, but they were having none of it. It was the porridge and the full breakfast, or it was nothing. With the glee of moral reckoning, Mary reported that when she ferried them to the trail, one of them fell asleep in her car and had to be pried out of the back seat. With much head shaking, Mary pronounced the shameful outcome: they were unable to complete the three-hour walk in less than seven. Where we could insert a word edgewise in this story, which was nowhere and required us to talk against the tide of Mary's voice, we agreed that walking on a full stomach was a taxing business.

Mary's way of talking was circuitous and repetitive, cultivating a jungle of verbosity occluding the central subject and harvesting the maximum amount of gab from the minimum amount of content. Since the monologue cycled rapidly, it was difficult to anticipate an end to the experience. We finally settled for walking away from the pub without waiting for a pause. Mary followed us to the middle of the road, talking the entire way. She seemed unperturbed as we waved goodbye and crossed the street, leaving her in mid-sentence.

We took refuge in J. F. O'Mahony's post office and general store, a well-worn village establishment where one can purchase anything or nothing, depending on whether they have what you want. Which, for the most part, they don't. As we entered, Frank O'Mahony, the proprietor, fixed me in the eye. With a look of concern, he asked, "Do you know the way to the nearest hospital?"

I felt the tug on my leg immediately, but his game was uncertain. I was sure that a winning response was impossible, so I chose caution. "There must be one in... Cork?"

This was an incorrect answer, and the question was repeated. "But do you know the way to the nearest hospital?"

Frank very much had the best of me and there was no way I could emerge with points for cleverness or wit. I muttered something idiotic about needing to return to the States to take advantage of my health insurance.

Frank, satisfied with his victory, provided the context. "But did you eat one of Mary's sandwiches?"

I looked at his face for a moment and burst out laughing. Here was the bard himself, serving up a satire in that sly, sharp way that no one does better than the Irish. I guess Frank judged that Mary was a subject safe enough for ridicule, but I wasn't so sure about that. It wouldn't surprise me if she made a few trips to the Poet's Well herself. Only later did it occur to me that I was the true object of the satire.

5

City Full of Dreams [Paris 2017-2018]

THE CAFÉ OF HUMAN KINDNESS [20th arrondissement]

It is certain that the café by itself with its patrons, its tables, its booths, its mirrors, its light, its smoky atmosphere, and the sounds of voices, rattling, saucers, and footsteps which fill it—the café is a fullness of being.

Jean-Paul Sartre, *Being and Nothingness*

It was a cold December day in Paris. The wind sliced down the narrow streets, hungry for bare skin. Stepping from the shelter of the apartment building, Susan and I shivered and tightened our scarves. Overhead, despite the blue sky, the sun brought little heat. But with no sign of rain, we chose to celebrate the day by walking to our favorite place. We had many favorite places, but this one, a café in a quiet neighborhood, embodied the things we loved most about the city.

We had discovered *Les Pitchettes* at the end of summer during one of our meandering rambles. Thirsty and hungry, we'd wanted refreshment and Susan, who has a knack for these things, spotted the café from across the street. Once inside, I saw what she had sensed. With mismatched furniture, a pastel color theme, North African music in the background, female staff, and—unusual for Paris—an immaculate bathroom, the café exuded charm. We inspected the menu, scrawled on a blackboard behind the counter. It reflected the discriminations of the proprietor, Madame Chaouach (shay-wook), a robust Algerian woman whose goodwill, we would learn, embraced all her customers. We savored the ambiance and the food, but on that first experience I needed to make sure before I could fully endorse the place. I performed the usual test: I ordered a cup of hot *chocolat*. Seasoned with chai spices, it arrived as a thick, black sludge so bitter that I added four sugar cubes. Even then, I felt like I was injecting it. In other words, it was perfect.

On that blustery day in December, *Les Pitchettes* offered a sanctuary from the wind, and we hurried into its steamy warmth. As we hunched over bowls of cooked grain, seeds, and leeks, we felt a rush of cold air when a young woman came through the door. A baby peeked out between the lapels of her greatcoat, and the woman pushed a stroller filled with groceries. There was no room for the stroller in the packed café, but without hesitation people scooted together and made space. The mother slipped into the last free table, unwound the infant from his swaddling, and began to nurse. Soon the waitress delivered a hot beverage and both mother and child settled in, content in their nourishment. In France, you'll hear no fuss about nursing in public; it's just life. They have an expression for such things: *c'est normal.* Literally, it means "it's normal," like we would say "it's all good." In France it means more than that, encompassing amusement and respect for the ways of the world, quirks and all.

Susan and I wiped our bowls with hunks of bread and smiled at each other, eager for dessert. Halfway through my viscous *chocolat*, mother and baby prepared to leave. When she stood to rewrap the child, I saw that he was plump and rosy. She handled him with care, securing him to her chest—facing out—with a long band of cloth, then kissed him a dozen times, each kiss delivered as a separate event. She approached the counter to pay while struggling with her coat. Susan rose and helped her into it and was rewarded with a blushing smile. The woman gave a bill to the cashier and turned to go, buttoning her coat around the child, leaving only his head exposed. He looked like a cherub borne by an angel. As they left, another woman on her way out pushed the stroller through the door, closely followed by the cashier, hand outstretched with a few coins of change. Once things were sorted outside, the cashier returned to deal with her other customers, who waited patiently because there's no hurry in a Parisian café. Bundled against the elements, the mother headed off down the street, pushing the stroller and leaning into the wind. She couldn't help it; she'd left behind some of her glow to mingle with the collective warmth in the café.

We kept returning to *Les Pitchettes*, even though it was a two mile walk from the apartment. When friends came to visit, we marched them straight there so they could sample the allure of Paris. Madame Chaouach couldn't seem to get enough of hugging and kissing her regular clients and gabbing with everyone who came through the door. We hadn't achieved the status of regulars although we were recognized and greeted joyfully. The last time we took friends to the café, I ordered the usual *chocolat*. All winter, I had been studying this beverage around the city, but nobody made it like they did at *Les Pitchettes*. The formula, if there was one, served as a template for the spontaneous creativity of the staff. I never had it the same way twice, not even close. This time, when it was carried out from behind the counter, in a beautiful green and gold cup with a tiny plate of dates and a ceramic box of brown sugar cubes, all arranged on a tray, it drew the attention of two other patrons. Madame Chaouach paused and dramatically held the tray under their noses so they could each inhale the aroma. I smiled at this scene, so typical of Parisian life, where the display and inspection of food is a public pastime. One of the inhalers saw me watching and called out *"pour vous?"* I nodded, she nodded, and it was like we knew each other.

Susan got a *panna cotta* topped with a green tomato confiture and almonds. She immediately proclaimed that it was the best thing she had ever eaten. When Susan asked about the ingredients of the confiture, Madame Chaouach said a few words we could understand and a few we could not. Giving up on words, she walked away. A few minutes later she returned with a pint jam jar filled with the confiture, which she presented to Susan, *"avec plaisir."* When we left, I offered to pay for it, but she shook her head, putting her hand over her heart and repeating that it was her pleasure. Then she and Susan kissed in that French way, cheek to cheek, both sides. As we walked out the door, I thought how much better it would be if the women of *Les Pitchettes* managed the great global café of humankind.

THE BONEYARD [5th arrondissement]

Daydream undoubtedly feeds on all kinds of sights, but through a sort of natural inclination, it contemplates grandeur. And this contemplation produces an attitude that is so special, an inner state that is so unlike any other, that the daydream transports the dreamer outside the immediate world to a world that bears the mark of infinity.

Gaston Bachelard, *The Poetics of Space*

In the foyer of the bone museum stands a massive, frightening sculpture. Crafted in life-like detail, the bronze portrays an orangutan throttling a human hunter, forcing the man down onto his back, twisted, helpless, and near death. The orangutan's infant stands at her side, eager to see the finale.

This grisly work can be found in the Gallery of Paleontology and Comparative Anatomy, one of a series of structures comprising the National Museum of Natural History in Paris. The museum covers the grounds of the seventy-acre *Jardin des Plantes*, a popular park on the Left Bank. Scattered through gardens formal and informal, greenhouses, monumental buildings, and a zoo, the museum offers a three-dimensional encyclopedia of the world. Walking across the street from the bustle of the Austerlitz metro station and into the park, you immediately encounter the Paleontology Gallery, an art nouveau exuberance of curved iron and glass. Its beauty entices; you want to go in. As soon as you cross the portal and see the raging primate, a disturbance settles over the mind. I'm certain it's a deliberate provocation. When Susan and I made our first visit to the Gallery, we eagerly lined up in the queue for the ticket booth. As we shuffled forward, the orangutan loomed over us; I couldn't take my eyes off it. I felt forced to reconsider the myth of human priority. And the subtext foreshadowed what lay ahead in the exhibit.

Tickets in hand, we escaped the foyer and slipped into the hall of comparative anatomy. Only a few feet in, I lost track of Susan. I stopped and turned slowly around, trying to position myself within the zodiac of visual riches. It was a matter of bones everywhere, all sizes and shapes, representing every type of animal on earth. My eyes came to rest on the wall above the entry where the curved jaws of whales were mounted like the triumphant scepters of a colossus. To left and right I saw glass cases crammed with bones and text, a marathon of scientific analysis impossible to fathom without hours of study. Ten feet into the exhibit and I felt overwhelmed. Taking a breath, I finished my rotation and faced the far end of the hall, at least a hundred yards away. I stared at what had stopped me in the first place: an onrushing horde of skeletons stretching the entire length of the space, an urgent assembly of all manner of beasts, frozen in a stampede toward the entry, or, from their perspective, the exit. Another provocation, as if to say, you may be alive, and we may be dead, but you'd better get the fuck out of the way.

    I craned and peered but failed to spot Susan through the overlapping layers of articulated bones. The narrow length of the hall drew me on, and I imagined Susan bounding ahead through the exhibit with the glee of discovery. In time, I knew the tortoise would catch the hare, so I plodded on, swiveling my head in the foolish attempt to see everything at once. I was captivated by the multi-paned windows that towered from just above the display cases to the ceiling. The windows, arched and ornate, filled the hall with light from both sides, illuminating the bones in shadowless glory. Graceful, exposed iron girders spanned the ceiling overhead. I could hardly choose between my awe at the room itself and what was in it. Finally, I narrowed my focus and studied the cases of anatomical exhibits collected from all over the world, a graphic display of the minutiae of comparative analysis. Full skeletons were displayed running, jumping, flying, crawling, and every other sort of activity with multiple examples of each. As I strolled by these cases I couldn't help but assume a scientific viewpoint, comparing and contrasting, marveling at the realms of similarity and difference. The exhibit labels, inscribed by hand, featured sensuous antique scripts that trespassed the boundaries of time. With the zeal of the analyst, I found myself comparing the faded ink and handwriting, trying to fix a chronology. In the end, I could only guess that many of the labels predated the building itself, over a century old. I caught up to Susan at the farthest reaches of the gallery, studying jars of preserved flesh—curiosities suitable for a carnival side show.

My eyes slid over these grotesque displays, preferring the clean, uncomplicated surfaces of bone.

Front to back, we'd already seen a thousand specimens and our heads were so stuffed with analysis that mine felt like a cotton ball. Yet there was more, much more. We climbed the worn wooden staircase to the second floor, pausing only to stand for a few moments on the balcony just below the ceiling. From this perch, we looked back down on the suspended blue whale skeleton and the diminutive human visitors milling around underneath. For a minute, I felt like an overlord reviewing his subjects.

That hubris lasted as long as it took to climb the rest of the way to the paleontology gallery. On this floor, the primary window covered the ceiling, where a single expanse of thick, green glass, supported by an iron grid, ran most of the length and width of the gallery. The darker tones of light filtering through the translucent roof matched the bones on exhibit, rich brown from their prolonged burials in the earth. The creatures in this hall were all extinct: mammoth, cave bear, Irish elk, and too many dinosaurs for comfort—a far-flung collection from the furry Ice Age to the reptilian Jurassic. No coordinated march of skeletons could be found here; each specimen stood apart, an ambassador from deep time. As we roamed the hall, I felt no grief at the loss of these creatures from field and woods; they were a scary lot. The strange Irish elk fascinated me with its rack the size of a dozer blade; it could take you out with a turn of the head.

The filmmaker Luc Besson used the paleontology gallery as a set in his fantasy, *The Extraordinary Adventures of Adele Blanc-Sec*, originally a series of popular graphic novels. An early scene in the film puts the viewer in the dinosaur exhibit, at night. A giant egg on display cracks, and a pterodactyl pecks through the shell. Breaking out, it launches and learns to fly by doing laps up and down the gallery. Despite the size of the room, it's hardly big enough for the enormous reptile, and before long it crashes through the ceiling pane and escapes into the city of Paris. Driven by hunger, it creates as much mayhem in the city as you might imagine and can only be tamed by the extraordinary Adele, who returns it to the museum, riding on its back through the sky. In her honor, the museum has placed a full-size cardboard cutout at the top of the exit staircase.

I've been attracted to old bones for most of my life, a legacy from my father, who took me on long walks in the desert. He could ramble across the near-empty sagebrush country for hours and hours without a sign of fatigue. Eyes to the ground, we scoured the terrain for agates, fossils, arrowheads—anything linked to the past. He treated these finds as sacraments and lacking any other religion, I followed his lead. Once, he placed a fossilized mammoth tooth in the palm of my hand and my mind slipped back ten thousand years. I could almost see the blue terminal walls of nearby glaciers and the herds of megafauna grazing the meadows lush from runoff. Now, when I find bones on walks in the wild, I always pick them up, and sometimes take them home, mesmerized by the shapes and weathered polish. A museum full of them was an ideal environment. Here I saw an abundance of sculptural bone, arranged with context, meaning, and artistic flourish.

True to its name, the museum embodies a variety of meanings associated with the word *gallery*: a long, narrow space, a balcony, and a room to display art. In this case, it's a place for science, but in France, that means it's also always about art. You find this in all their science displays. Aesthetics, through precision of image and arrangement, convey a clarity of thought without negating the transcendent dimensions of knowing. For example, in the gallery of comparative anatomy, you can study the carefully articulated bones as closely as you like, but it never removes the anticipation of being trampled under a charging horde. No matter how ossified the beasts, a vestige of spirit lingers within.

Paris is full of famous museums, but we had no interest in the Louvre, D'Orsay, or the other hallmarks. Instead, we kept returning to the gardens and glass of Muséum national d'Histoire naturelle. During our second visit, I climbed up to the highest balcony, just under the leaf and grime-stained translucence of the second-floor ceiling. I'd neglected this area before, overcome by museum fatigue. I was surprised to find that the balcony, which circumvented the entire space below of paleontology specimens, featured cases exhibiting the oldest of all life-forms: fossils of plants and sea creatures hundreds of millions of years old. Humans and other mammals occupied no place in this menagerie. Thus, as you ascend through the space of the building, you move further and further back in time, until, at the uppermost level just below the sky itself, you encounter the oldest beings. The museum functions as a time machine that drags the visitor back through layers of earthly biology, back to the origin of life on the planet, whispering along the way that, after all, humans don't occupy much space in the grand cavalcade of existence.

We left the building and Susan wandered off to photograph an old-fashioned carousel in the garden. I walked along the exterior of the bone gallery, looking back inside through the windows, still entranced with the skulls and arched spines of the running skeletons. Long dead, perhaps, but I could swear they moved, and I stared hard to hold them still, until I grew tired with the impossible task of reining in my imagination. Reluctantly, I let them fade and turned my attention to a bronze statue standing between the building and the surrounding hedge. I had to stretch on my toes to get a full view over the greenery. The sculpture showed a paleolithic man with a carving knife in one hand, and a look of rapture on his face. In the outstretched palm of his other hand was a delicate carving of a mammoth, an offering to the ages of passers-by. How apt this image, a counterpoint to the man in the foyer dying at the hands of a vengeful orangutan. Here was man the artist, demonstrating humble respect for the animals rather than presumptions of dominance. We know how to do this, the sculpture suggests, and we'd be better off if we did. Instead of relegating our fellow inhabitants of the earth to the status of *other*, we should build temples of understanding and find our place in the commune of life. Or is our vaunted intelligence nothing more than a bigger tooth or a sharper claw?

NAKED ON THE TARMAC [20th arrondissement]

...moderation has never appeared to me the hall-mark of a vigorous artistic nature.

Charles Baudelaire, "Richard Wagner and Tannhäuser in Paris"

Freedom is its own nothingness.

Jean-Paul Sartre, *The War Diaries*

Paris has an energetic theatre culture encompassing every style of performance known to the stage. During our year in the city, Susan and I initially shied away from sampling the offerings, given our rudimentary command of the language. Curiosity finally got the better of us and we decided to try a show that appeared to be more dance than word. That seemed like a safe choice.

The venue, like many in Paris, was well designed and maintained, a lovely example of the city's commitment to culture. Located just down the street from our apartment, every time we walked past *Le Tarmac* to get to our favorite bakery, we stopped and inspected the display of dramatic posters. They specialized in artists from every part of the "francophone" world—a large catchment given the historical ambitions of French colonialism.

We purchased tickets online for a show titled "*Néant,*" a French word which can be translated as "nothingness." Jean-Paul Sartre wrangled with the philosophical contortions of this term in his doorstop volume *Being and Nothingness.* I'm not sure why we ignored this blatant clue regarding the nature of our show, but we did. Perhaps we felt some affinity with the performer —Dave St-Pierre from Quebec—since we shared a continent with him.

On the evening of the performance, we walked smartly to the theater, excited to see advanced culture in our own neighborhood. Once in the lobby we milled around with the other sophisticates, a mixed-age crowd clad in the casual but stylish fashion that is a hallmark of Parisians. We hoped no one would initiate a conversation, forcing us to reveal that we were Americans with an unsophisticated grasp of French. As the time approached for the show to start, we kept glancing at the doors to the auditorium, wondering when they would let us inside. At eight o'clock one of the doors opened a crack and a man slipped out, closing it behind him.

He was a short, bearded man wearing a flat clothing bag, like one might receive from the dry cleaners. Though hindered by the bag, he waddled around the lobby, mixing with the crowd, and chatting merrily. He wore a long, curly blonde wig and spoke in an affected falsetto. Except for the clothing bag, which was clear plastic and concealed nothing, he was naked. He made a point of talking to everyone, occasionally stopping to shout announcements. We didn't understand him very well because he spoke in rapid French. He stopped to talk with us, but we were too tongue-tied to sustain his interest. He moved on, leaving us to speculate about what the hell was going on. Susan suggested that this was some sort of warm-up act but, of course, it was the show itself.

After twenty minutes of this confusion, the doors opened wide and we all streamed into the seats, the man in the bag included. The theater was technically impressive, with a large, well-equipped stage and tiered rows to accommodate two or three hundred spectators. We settled into comfortable seats in the fifth row. The bag man sat behind us in the middle of the audience and while we alternated between staring at the empty stage and craning our heads around, he talked at length, maintaining the falsetto, driving himself to one histrionic crescendo after another. I only understood a few phrases, like *"completement absurde"* and *"cette merde."* For the most part, I refrained from turning around to look at him as he was only two rows back. I didn't want to catch his eye for fear of what could happen. It was crystal clear that there would be no boundaries within this "nothingness."

I have no idea how long he sat in the audience and harangued us; it seemed to go on forever. As he raved, I noticed that I started to understand more of his French, no doubt a survival mechanism on my part. Eventually he pranced—I mean that literally—down the aisle and onto the stage. I relaxed a little at that point, considering it movement toward a norm. The stage was huge, but he inhabited it like a second home, continuing the monologue and vamping with the enthusiasm of an eight-year-old at a costume party. This was apparently hilarious because the audience was in stitches. At one point he stood on the edge of the stage, clutched his member, and started masturbating. This was also met with gales of laughter. He kept at it beyond any reasonable limit, thankfully stopping before soiling the inside of his bag.

Having apparently exhausted the things he could do with his own equipment, he introduced props, notably two six-foot-long inflatable penises. They were the same pink color as Pepto-Bismol. He selected an audience member to join him on stage, a young woman who giggled incessantly. He dared her to kiss a plastic penis suspended from the ceiling by a cord, egging her on while he playfully batted it at her face. She giggled so hard that she seemed on the verge of vibrating into thin air. Giving up on her inability to provide anything but nervous laughter, he waved her off the stage.

For the next scene, he lined up five inflatable deer and asked the audience to name them. A woman in our row kept yelling out "*Don-Ald Trump*" but despite her enthusiasm the creatures ended up with names like "Hortense" and "Amelie." M. St-Pierre, the performer, expressed great fondness for the deer. He patted them, hugged them, and couldn't stop talking about how sweet they were. Then, in a fit of puckish glee, he let all the air out of the fake animals, eulogizing them as they evaporated on the stage. He was grief-struck beyond all recourse.

We considered leaving, but as we were near the front and in the middle of the row, our departure would not have gone unnoticed. The punishment for such a betrayal would have been some form of public humiliation, we had no doubt, so we settled in for the duration, committed to the complete experience of nothingness.

The theater suddenly darkened, and dry ice smoke rolled across the stage. Our host shed the wig and the plastic bag to emerge in the final perfection of his nudity. A pounding electronic soundtrack occupied every cubic inch of air space, enhanced by a synchronized light show illuminating the smoke. No longer mincing the mock feminine, he strode around the stage with muscular aggression slowed to a ritual pace. He had become an intense, brooding, primordial mythologem of masculinity exhumed from the Freudian unconscious. Like everything else about the performance, this went on long past the point of fading novelty. I developed a concern that the fast pulse of the deafening soundtrack would precipitate a cardiac event, if not in me, then some other unfortunate spectator. Abruptly, he stopped, shedding the posture of an id-monster, and the lights came up. He donned the blonde wig and resumed the falsetto identity. That, however, was not the end.

Next, he launched into a critique of the lack of meaning in his show. He paused his analysis to ask for another volunteer. To my amazement, and despite the preceding events, there were no shortage of applicants. He selected a young man and challenged him to ascend the stage and provide an improvised lecture about theatrical meaning, or something like that. The volunteer started off well, but our master of ceremonies waved a hand and disco music blasted over the sound system. As he bounced to the beat, M. Floppy Cock urged the volunteer to forget about the lecture and perform a strip tease instead. The fellow agreed and began to disrobe with an embarrassing surfeit of enthusiasm, grinding to the music as if he'd always wanted to do this. He didn't get very far before the performer cut him off, perhaps wary of being upstaged. The volunteer, shooed back into the audience, was then berated for lowering the standards of the performance. After delivering this plenary judgment, the performer threw the giant plastic penises into our midst and encouraged us to bounce them back and forth over our heads while he gyrated on stage to the sounds of the leftover disco music. The audience was happy to oblige. Susan and I cringed but had no choice except to play along, batting away the grotesque balloons whenever they flew at our faces.

Following this segment, the id-monster returned, with more smoke and the industrial noise soundtrack. There were differences this time, though I couldn't explain what they meant. He stomped and dominated the stage with the kinetics of myth and ritual—I got that much. I'm sure this was the "dancing" part of the performance. It was compelling in a way, if only because there was nothing to do but inspect every square inch of his sweaty body, sort of like an anatomy lesson.

Like clockwork, after this segment the blonde wig returned for a while, followed by the monster, and then he went back and forth between these two formats, sort of a sacred and profane thing, I suppose, for 2 1/2 hours. During one of the profane sections, he borrowed several audience cellphones to take close-up selfies of his penis, crowing about how the owners of the phones would forever cherish these souvenirs. I wasn't so sure about that; at any rate, by the end of the performance, who needed a photograph? We got to know his penis as if it were our own. Eventually, in the blonde mode, he resumed his seat two rows behind us, sitting quietly. It could have been the ending, though no one seemed certain enough to leave. The silence in the theater was as embarrassing as anything we'd already endured. Perhaps exhausted from his elaboration of nothing, M. St-Pierre resolved uncertainty by announcing that the show was over, and people should go.

To say that we left the theater stunned would be an understatement. Thereafter, when we walked past *Le Tarmac* on the way to the bakery, we ignored the posters and didn't even talk about seeing another show. The very idea was absurd.

LAIR OF THE ANARCHISTS [20th arrondissement]

*City of swarming, city full of dreams
Where ghosts in daylight tug the stroller's sleeve!*

Charles Baudelaire, "The Seven Old Men"

Walking the streets of Paris with my wife—as I did for hours every day—required patience and humility. Don't get me wrong —we were both culprits of distraction. We might set out at the same pace, but before long, one of us would see something that compelled an immediate halt. The other often sailed on, oblivious, until the mate was missed. Then came the slow turn, the puzzled look, or, at bad moments, the glare, followed by a trudge back to see what was so important. When we could, we held hands while we strolled, but the sidewalks were crowded, narrow, and difficult to navigate as a single, let alone a duo.

The personal tangents reflected our curiosities. For Susan, it might be a thrift shop or an art display and for me a bakery or an informational plaque. We tried to cultivate an amused tolerance for each other's whims. It pleased me to learn that many clothing boutiques supplied a chair in front of the store for husbands— no entry required. Since watching people go by is the best diversion in Paris, waiting was hardly a punishment. However, it wasn't all push and pull—we shared enough interests to make each walk an adventure of common exploration. For example, neither of us, during our long residence, passed a bookstore without stopping.

Another shared enthusiasm: we always scrutinized the new posters. Pasted and taped to free surfaces, sometimes, like wallpaper, several layers thick, posters adorn all the main streets of the 20th arrondissement. It's an important form of communication in the nontouristic parts of the city—another venue of social media. Each announcement reflects a new matter for social consideration: lost-cat placards, advertisements for flea markets and other neighborhood gatherings, performances professional and amateur, political advice, and scattered one-off graphic art installations so surrealistic that it's impossible to understand their functions. Performance posters tend to be bold, guaranteed to draw your attention. These are direct communications between promoters and pedestrians, urging people to come hear the music, see the play, join the dance, or go on strike. When political posters aren't associated with specific events, they resemble the venting common to online forums, only a bit more thoughtful. A favorite target is President Emmanuel Macron, frequently depicted as Napoleon because he is short and imperious. Many people consider posters to be eyesores, hence the prevalence of "POST NO BILLS" or, as it's written in France, "*défense d'afficher*," which means "protected against affixing." Despite the widespread proscriptions, I believe bill posting to be a manifestation of democracy. A large audience is guaranteed and for little investment your message, no matter how mundane or how weird, can be put in front of every pedestrian.

We learned things from reading the posters, such as who was making music at what theater or club, information that we weren't getting elsewhere. These words on the street also introduced us to the diversity of political factions in Paris. The city harbors extremists and rebels of every sort, especially on the left. Although rowdy at times, these cadres prefer argument to violence, unlike the terrorists who circulate in the shadows. Two years before our visit, Islamic State operatives attacked the Bataclan theater and killed ninety people at a rock concert. With that and other terrorist acts haunting the public memory, the city remained on alert. We often saw soldiers on the streets in patrols of six, armed with full combat gear. I surprised myself by welcoming their presence; both Susan and I failed to bristle because we felt safer, whether we were or not. One day as we sat in a café, a military patrol sauntered by and a woman at the next table looked at us, shrugged, and said *"C'est Paris, n'est-ce pas?"* The Gallic nonchalance was infectious. *"Bien sûr,"* we replied and stopped worrying about being slaughtered in the city we loved.

New posters went up every day. During one of our neighborhood rambles, I spied a startling addition pasted on a bare stretch of wall. The text recommended that workers initiate an immediate general strike because "your right to work is well worth a general strike." It depicted exuberant workers waving flags against a background of exploding red and black rays emanating from an unknown revolutionary source just over the horizon. The primary colors, red and black, proclaimed affinity with traditional anarchism. The design elements reminded me of the constructivist motifs perfected by the Soviets in their poster art of the 20s and 30s. At the Stedelijk Museum in Amsterdam, I had been lucky enough to see a print of a masterpiece in this genre, the 1931 Soviet poster titled "Let's build a fleet of airships in Lenin's name!" Against a sky full of giant, phallic zeppelins Lenin looms at attention, nobly paternal. Underneath the genius of revolution stands a mob of cheering workers who can't wait to get to the factory and start work. Some would consider this kitsch, I suppose, but the brashness of it thrilled me beyond explanation.

I saw the same brazen style echoed in the general strike poster. It gleamed like a beacon across the street, and I jaywalked for a closer look. In the lower corner was a picture of a hissing black cat, back arched, fur standing on end. Definitely an old anarchist symbol, a warning to the capitalists. Don't tread on me, it suggests, or I'll scratch your eyes out. Inscribed on the body of the cat were three letters: CNT. I stared in wonder. The Confederacion Nacional del Trabajo (National Confederation of Labor) was one of the oldest anarcho-syndicalist groups in existence. Founded in Barcelona in 1910, they played a major role in the revolutionary Catalonian state of the 30s and the desperate Civil War that followed, fighting to defend the republic against Franco and his fascist allies. Following Franco's victory in 1939, many Spaniards fled to France, bringing their politics and traditional culture. They went underground during the Nazi Occupation, but they were a tough bunch and survived the war. Now here they were, still demanding general strikes, somewhat quixotically, I thought, as the business of the streets went on, unheeding the call.

I first learned about the CNT as a teenager. During those years I read many books, but three emerged as instrumental, nudging me toward a career as social misfit. Thoreau's *Walden* taught me that the only shelter I needed was a coffin-size box, Kerouac's *The Dharma Bums* showed me that I didn't even need that but could just crash on people's floors, and Orwell's *Homage to Catalonia* finished the job by convincing me that the usual apparatus of the state made it impossible to find enough peace for any sort of dwelling. Even though my parents loved me, and I had few adverse childhood experiences except for the loss of my dog when I was six, Orwell's book front-loaded a predisposition toward resentment. An urgent and compelling memoir, it had sucked up my naïveté and transported it right along with the author to fight against fascism in Spain. Desperate to enter the fray and failing to understand the complexities of the factions, Orwell signed with the POUM, a fringe group of Trotskyite Marxists. Since Stalin had made it a priority to exterminate Trotsky and all his supporters, this was a dangerous affiliation. I choked on my idealism as I read how its own partisans, notably the Communists, undermined the republic; the Reds would rather lose than support the success of Trotskyites and anarchists. A wounded Orwell narrowly escaped Spain with his life, while his optimism lay shattered in the remains of democratic endeavor. The experience left him wary of authoritarian tendencies on both the Right and the Left, a concern that reached memorable expression more than a decade later in his novel *1984*.

This is the kind of stuff that had been sloshing around in my head for fifty years. Viewing the CNT logo brought it back, infusing me with an unearned pride of solidarity, a sentiment still looking for validation in my unrevolutionary life. Eager for more encounters with living history, I scouted the streets like a dog. I soon learned that Paris was filled with CNT propaganda.

Especially in the 20th *arrondissement*, our neighborhood, the most radical district of the city. The last, fatal stand of the Paris Commune in 1871 happened a mile away from our apartment in the Père Lachaise cemetery. There's a monument on the interior wall, where the rebels were lined up and shot. Always I saw bundles of flowers by the dozen gracing this spot, tagged by unions and other worker organizations who didn't want to forget, and haven't forgotten, the utopian dreams of a hundred and fifty years ago.

I collected the posters that I liked, cultural and political, depending on the ease of their removal. My ethics were simple; I only took down posters for lapsed events or those in danger of being covered over with fresh layers. As much as I wanted the garish CNT propaganda, I found it daunting to salvage. The canny radicals had learned to apply their products with high-grade paste on permanent-stick surfaces like concrete or plaster. Run-of-the-mill advertising settled for a lower standard. One day I caught a billposter plying the craft of slap and dash. He double-parked his car, jumped out, grabbed a bucket of paste and a mop from the back seat, swabbed over some existing posters, literally slapped up a row of new ones, threw the materials back in the car, and roared off in a flurry of horns from blocked traffic. Sometimes tape and staples provided substitute adhesive—good for me because I could simply slice or pry with Susan's handy Opinel pocketknife. However, CNT posters bonded with the vertical substrate of the city itself. They could only be removed by scraping and tearing the paper, bit by bit—a method that left nothing to collect but shreds. Despite my steadily increasing hoard of street art, the lack of CNT material left me frustrated.

I prowled and scanned relentlessly, hoping to find the fluke. But I never did.

We often walked down the hill to the southern part of the 20th *arrondissement*; it's a cozy part of the city with our favorite café and an absence of known tourist attractions. Sequences of dead-end alleys perforate the interior of blocks outlined by narrow streets. An alley is called an *impasse* and can bear a colorful name like *Poule* (prostitute) or *Souhaits* (wishes), but my favorite is *Impasse Satan*. One day, as we strolled along a new route to the café, I realized that we were seeing a high concentration of CNT posters. No doubt I drove Susan nuts with all the stopping and starting as I dashed from propaganda to propaganda, but I couldn't help it in the face of such a motherlode. Luckily, she indulged this compulsion.

Halfway along a block of the *rue des Vignoles* (street of vineyards), I stopped short at the entrance to an unnamed *impasse*. It wasn't quaint like most of the others, instead it was dirty, in a funky sort of way, and reminded me of the old, decayed sections of Seattle before that city lost its dilapidated charms to gentrified coffee. The alley harbored two-story spaces built out of cheap materials like plywood and single-pane glass. Doors lined both sides, but they didn't look like apartment entries. I wanted to know what lay behind those doors. CNT placards, posters, and announcements covered all the available wall spaces. An enclave for the hardcore, no doubt about it. My lame command of French reminded me that I'd be unable to explain myself should anyone ask. Desperate with curiosity, I wanted to walk down the *impasse*, but it didn't look like a public way and timidity triumphed. We moved on, while I berated myself for passing by an obvious anarchist lair.

Back at our apartment, the internet's goofy translations eventually provided answers to the questions on my mind. The place we found wasn't just any old lair, it was the French headquarters of the CNT. *Voila*. I had to get in.

We soon returned to the lower 20th, determined to penetrate the sanctum. No matter what happened, I figured we could retreat to the café of kindness, two blocks away. With that in mind, I cautiously advanced down the alley of the anarchists, still uneasy that someone might challenge us as interlopers. The place seemed deserted. We came to the end of the passage and stopped at the door to the CNT office. It didn't look very official. I peered through the dirty window, straining to see the interior where nothing moved in the dim light. The door was unlocked. In fact, it didn't exactly fit in the frame and couldn't close properly, which was how I knew it was unlocked. I studied an assortment of hasps screwed onto the door; it looked possible to force the mating parts together, but now they hung in disarray. The sign on the door said that the office (they called it an *atelier*, or "workshop") was open for a five-hour period once a week. Not exactly what I expected for the national headquarters of a vast anarchist propaganda machine. Apparently, changing the world didn't involve extensive office hours. Dejected, we turned and walked back toward the street. I took the opportunity to study the posters along the walls and discovered a section devoted to ads for flamenco activities. Part of the Spanish heritage, I thought. Right here in the compound you could attend performances and take lessons in singing or dancing. Susan had shared her love of flamenco early in our relationship and now we were both fans, drawn to the energy and passion. An earthy expression of dignity within suffering, of course it has a place in the revolution. Just like Emma Goldman said: "If I can't dance, I don't want to be part of your revolution."

My new plan called for boldness; I would go to the CNT office during the brief time that it claimed to be open and beg for posters. Even though my request might seem odd, and my French skills would be insufficient to convince otherwise, I perceived no alternative. At this point the whole quest had become one of those pursuits that stoked, rather than calmed, the obsession. If things went badly, the nearby café had hot chocolate and cake.

Before I could visit the *atelier* during business hours, we returned to the alley and saw a flamenco performance. We arrived early on a rainy night, purchased tickets, and found places close to the stage. The seating was modest: metal folding chairs arranged in loose rows with a long center aisle. As we waited, I studied the architecture. I decided that the room used to be a warehouse or garage. Exposed wiring dangled like cobwebs. A small fortune in duct tape decorated every surface in the venue; it seemed to be the default adhesive. The high ceiling, what there was of it, consisted of mismatched materials such as plywood and plasterboard tacked up along the rafters to cover some, but far from all, of the fiberglass insulation. Several batts had pulled away and hung in space. I detected no heating system. Clearly, the building existed beyond the ken of code enforcement.

It didn't take long to fill to capacity, a hundred or more. The audience consisted mostly of older Spanish women dressed for the evening, all holding paper plates full of *charcuterie* and cheese, and drinking wine out of plastic cups. The women gabbed in lively groups, ready to party. Everyone seemed to know each other. Susan and I exchanged looks and felt like true foreigners; if our French was bad, our Spanish was nonexistent. We slid up against the wall to make room for these energetic elders. My shoulder chilled quickly against the uninsulated wall. The room, however, grew warm with the excitement of body heat. We heard the performers loosening up in the back with guitar strumming and a frenzy of clacking heels. Suspense tingled through the audience like downed electrical wires, and we were eager for the show. Finally, the performers emerged from their cloister and paraded up the center aisle. Two male guitar players climbed on to the platform and sat in folding chairs side by side, stage right. Then, two male singers, with movements of studied grace, placed themselves on the left. These men had jet black hair and moody faces. The dancer was last to ascend, a powerful-looking woman wearing a black dress and a red scarf, the anarchist colors. She centered herself, a few notes sounded from the guitars and the stage exploded in a frenzy of music and movement. A rough passion flooded through me, channeling the anguish of a thousand years, wrenching it out of the collective soul and flinging it bravely to the floor, holding nothing back.

Eschewing delicacy for energy, the singers cast a torrent of agony into the air, the guitarists strummed out a ground of agile, driving rhythms, and at the center, the dancer's gravity pulled everything to her. Whirling, strutting, stomping, arms flying, she was a thunderstorm of pride, grief, and love. She was holy. The audience worshipped loudly, constantly exclaiming "*Olé!*" imbuing that term with personal nuance of adulation. Repeatedly, I heard the dancer's name called, *"Aurelia!"* sometimes in a shout, sometimes spoken softly as if the word escaped the lips in spontaneous awe.

We were enthralled, astonished with it all, from the surroundings to the performance, and we gladly wrapped ourselves in it. Sweat rolled down Aurelia's neck, drenching her garments, but she looked like she could go all night. Eventually, though, the audience needed a break, and after a last burst like the finale of fireworks, the music and dancing crashed to an end. Ovations followed as the performers retreated down the aisle. We slipped out through the excited crowd, into the cool, moist night, and walked home, savoring the richness of the experience. We said our thanks to the streets of Paris for harboring these refugees and making room for some free Spaniards.

Fueled by the spirit of anti-fascist flamenco, we marched down to the CNT *atelier* during its scheduled hours. The unlocked door presented no obstacle to entry, and we surveyed the room from just past the threshold. It looked like every other hard luck left-wing sanctuary. The layout featured a long table surrounded by an assortment of chairs in one quarter, cluttered desks scattered around the other quarters, another table, and along the walls and between the stations were racks and shelves of books and pamphlets. Comfortable chaos prevailed. A man sitting at the big table looked up from his sandwich, nodded in resignation, carefully replaced the sandwich on a paper plate, and walked over to see what we wanted. As we began fumbling toward a conversation, another fellow wandered in from a back room. He resembled the first guy: long, stringy hair, full beard, rumpled shirt, and faded jeans. I placed us all in the same faded generation. Their command of English was no better than ours of French, so we went back and forth, trying to cobble together enough lingo to talk. When they found out that we were Americans, their interest perked up. I wondered how many American tourists had ever walked through that door.

With some effort I got across my request for posters. Raising an eyebrow, one guy pulled a tube of paper off a shelf and unrolled it in front of me. I nodded. *"Oui, comme ca."* He laid it on the nearest table and grabbed another. *"Exactement,"* I said for encouragement. Meanwhile, the other anarchist roamed off to various corners of the office, returning with posters and thrusting them into my hands. Without hesitation, they expanded the treasure hunt, excavating through piles and shelves of material, hauling in batches of posters, stickers, and assorted graphics. It wasn't long before an imposing stack of propaganda sat on the table.

Trying to enlarge the conversation, I told them, possibly in a way that they understood, that I had once worked in a leftist collective in the States and that I supported their syndicalist ideas. Some part of this must have sunk in because they shifted their tactics and unloaded a barrage of everything they could find written in English: brochures, radical magazines from five years ago, even a copy of *Durruti: The People Armed*, a book about a CNT hero of the Spanish Civil War. I said no to the Durruti book since I had read it many years ago, which highlighted my credibility, perhaps. I started to question what I was going to do with all this stuff. I offered them a financial contribution to defray the costs of future printing, which they eagerly accepted. However, that led to a fresh round of proffered goods. I was led into the alley and down several doors where we entered a musty, disorganized room full of books and posters. The anarchist proceeded to pull out several high-quality prints to add to the trove. One was a Cartier-Bresson photograph used to promote a show of radical art. As we mulled over posters in the small storeroom, I couldn't help but notice my benefactor's pronounced body odor. Perhaps he hadn't had his weekly bath. I could care less; an ecstasy of solidarity dampened my sensitivities. These guys reminded me of the grungy radicals I had known in Seattle. To live free, you have to let go of a few things.

We left with a load of treasure and a warm feeling for our new comrades. The grungy little *impasse* had grounded our fantasies of Spanish anarchy and flamenco. I appreciated that no matter how dreamy my own sympathies, others lived them as reality. Utopian visions are fragile and require the continuous investment of love and energy. Not just another blind alley, the CNT enclave provided a nest for writing, printing, singing, and dancing, all in the name of believing in a better world.

Susan and I joked about how there would be no way I could get my suitcase through American customs, crammed with Palestinian scarves and anarchist posters. Determined to bring home these artifacts of the Parisian streets, these elemental touchstones of our rambling, I rolled the posters into a cardboard tube and buried it in my luggage along with the accumulated mementoes of a year abroad. When the time came, for whatever reason, we and our giant bags sailed through customs. True, George Orwell wouldn't have been impressed by the scope of this deed, but I've never been as virtuous as my heroes. I keep thinking I owe something to the anarchists back in the lair, though. There must be a way to get the word out. I've thought about plastering the walls of our town with the posters—create a little agitation for social change—but I think the impact would be minimal. They're all written in French.

DESIRING MACHINES [3rd arrondissement]

...the machine is desire—but not because desire is desire of the machine but because desire never stops making a machine in the machine....

Gilles Deleuze and Feliz Guattari, *Kafka: Toward A Minor Literature*

In the opening scene of Umberto Eco's *Foucault's Pendulum*, a novel of conspiracies and the occult, the protagonist seeks a place to hide in the exhibits of the *Musée des Arts et Métiers*, the Parisian museum of crafts and technology. He's frantic to be out of sight before closing time when the guards do their rounds. As we read, caught up in his desperation, we learn why. At midnight, an obscure cult plans to infiltrate the museum and sacrifice a friend of the protagonist in a ritual that will alter the world—not for the better. Our hero maintains no hope to save his friend from the powerful cult, but he wants to witness the event, if only to prove to himself that he hasn't imagined the conspiracy and its sinister agenda. The novel tells this story in a tangle of convoluted plots, murder, secret societies, fraud, maniacs, semiotic erudition, sex, and mayhem. With the museum, Eco picked a perfect stage for the critical scenes of the novel; aside from the presence of the famous pendulum, which he imagines as the focus of the cult's deranged metaphysics, the museum also displays, in detail, the machine obsessions that lurk at the boundaries of science and the occult.

French culture encompasses a high regard for science. During the frenzy of the Revolution, the radicals cast off the yoke of religion and replaced it with the secular values of the Enlightenment. Energies that once built soaring cathedrals were redirected toward the creation of new sanctums that taught science and worshipped art. In some cases, the hallowed structures of the religious class were simply flushed of their contents and recreated as temples of learning. The once-mighty Parisian priory of *Saint-Martin-des-Champs* went through such a transformation. Long an example of the political power of the Church, the priory grew wealthy from unearned acquisitions, a history that galled the Revolutionaries. In 1790, the State seized the priory and used it to incarcerate enemies of the Revolution. Twelve years later, to celebrate the rationalism of the State, the compound was changed into a museum for scientific technology, evicting God once and for all and clearing space for human creations, the machines.

On our visit to the museum, it was a typical rainy day in Paris, and we were more interested in scooting into the shelter of the building than in admiring the drops channeling down its seven-hundred-year-old Gothic exterior. We checked our wet jackets in the coatroom and walked down a hall to enter the great round apse of the chapel. There I experienced a child-like paralysis of excitement. On display were antique devices of science, crafted with a fine-tuned aesthetic and love of clockwork precision. Each one sat on a pedestal, echoing the stance of altars in the former church. I felt giddy—it was as if I had walked into a cover of the pulp science fiction magazines I collected in my youth.

Foucault's famous pendulum swung on a hundred-and-fifty-foot cable from the pinnacle of the domed ceiling. Once I noticed it, I ignored everything else, mesmerized by its mystery and power. The business end of the pendulum is a ten-inch metal ball swooping back and forth above the surface of a calibrated circle on the floor. Hash marks around the periphery of the twelve-foot circle divide it into sections of arc and a pointer fixed to the bottom of the ball allows you to observe exactly where it crosses the circle coming and going, seemingly in perpetual motion. As a safety precaution, a low fence cordons off the device and prevents a distracted visitor from getting bashed. I registered the specific intersections of pendulum and circle, just to mark the variance over time. And it did vary! The plane of the swing gradually shifted around the circle. Not in front of my eyes; I don't have that much patience. But I checked it again on the way out and, sure enough, it crossed the circle at different points. Léon Foucault's idea in 1851 showed that the earth rotates on an axis and proved it for all time. I've read explanations of why this demonstration proves the matter, but try as I might, I don't understand them. When I summoned my wits to imagine the mechanics of the pendulum, inexorably swinging backwards and forwards in space while the chapel rotated independently along with the surface of the earth, I ended up with a headache.

According to scientific history, the issue was settled in the nineteenth century; that's good enough for me. I was content to let the device beguile me with its irresistible arcs, back and forth, back and forth.

At the climax of Eco's novel, Foucault's Pendulum becomes the instrument of a grisly murder, which made me think of other pendulum assisted crimes. I instantly recalled the 1961 Roger Corman film based on Edgar Allan Poe's story "The Pit and the Pendulum." I saw it at a tender age over the objections of my mother, who feared I would have nightmares. In the film, an obsessed fanatic, played by Vincent Price, has a fondness for torturing everyone he can lay his hands on. In the climax, the hero, too late to save his sister from the madman, loses his struggle with Price and wakes up to find himself lashed to a stone slab. The slab sits under a razor-sharp blade fixed to the end of a long wooden arm that swings to and fro, dropping lower with each arc, inexorably descending toward the goal of dividing our hero's body into separate halves. Most disturbing is the "whoosh" noise the blade makes as it passes the low point of each arc. Just as my mother predicted, the movie gave me nightmares for months. In the museum, I was relieved that Foucault's Pendulum did not "whoosh" but remained mute.

Shaking off the spell of tortured memory, not to mention science, we proceeded from the apse to the nave of the repurposed church. Here the original utilitarian elements of worship had also been removed. No pews, no altars, no icons, nothing to suggest a Christian origin. Instead, it was filled with an array of giant steam engines and steam-powered machines, all polished to a sanctified gleam. Lurking in the shadows at the back stood

Frédéric Bartholdi's ten-foot-high original model of the Statue of Liberty.

Three stories of open scaffolding improbably occupied half the floor space of the nave. We hiked up the scaffold stairs, stopping at each level to inspect the old automobiles and other technological artifacts on display. The scaffolding provided low railings to prevent the visitor from plunging over the edge to the stone floor; since the railings barely cleared my knees, I doubted their effectiveness. At the top level of the scaffold, we stood even with two airplanes suspended from the ceiling. These flying machines were products of the dawn of aviation and appeared to be made from average household materials. No doubt, they served to advance the cause of aeronautics, but they looked so fragile that, rather than fly in one, I'd prefer being dragged about Troy behind the chariot of Achilles. Simply being on the top level of the scaffold gave me vertigo. The proximity to the airplanes, far from reassuring, just emphasized the distance to the bone-crunching stones below. I felt a worrisome sway in the scaffolding when another visitor tromped up the stairs. Certain that if I even tried to walk around on the quivering platform, I would stagger and pitch over the railing, I feigned boredom and sat on the steps, where I waited for Susan to conclude her aerial photography.

As we explored further into the museum, I noted the Gallic fondness for steampunk. This term denotes a type of science fiction that romanticizes the quaint glories of Victorian aesthetics. In steampunk speculations, Belle Epoque and art nouveau styles dominate and technology is driven by the power of steam. The classic representative of this fictional style remains Jules Verne, even though, being embedded in the original era, he could not reflect on it with the same irony as modern practitioners. Verne was enamored of technological possibility as well as aesthetics and through his massively popular novels, he shaped a fashion of machine reality. Verne failed to attain admission to the Pantheon, but he is still honored. The Metro station underneath the museum echoes Verne and his ethos. It features curved, riveted walls with a bronze sheen and heavy inset portholes that make you feel like you're inside the Nautilus submarine from *Twenty Thousand Leagues Under the Sea*. And surely, it's no coincidence that while Verne's *Nautilus* prowled the oceans of the world and served as the obsessive Captain Nemo's submersible museum, the *Musée des Arts et Métiers* itself is a giant chambered nautilus transporting through time the artifacts of human obsession.

We strolled through room after room filled with the components of a dreaming technology. One room contained nothing but gears and pistons of every sort and size, polished to brilliance and enclosed in cases of sparkling glass like sacred relics. Another room displayed the all-important mechanisms of couture: sewing machines for all uses, industrial and domestic. From there we walked on, into a chamber of lathes, the machine that makes other machines. Every material surface glowed with the promises of technological faith. We ended up in a side room crammed with 19th century automatons: detailed, toy-like machines capable of sound and movement, articulated dolls that you could crank into motion if you wanted to scare the daylights out of someone. Each automaton exuded an inherent creepiness that again reminded me of horror films I'd seen and wished I hadn't.

Unlike the characters in those films, who always ignored the cues of impending doom, we left before things got really weird.

Delight replaced dis-ease when we turned a corner and saw a full-scale replica of a flying machine devised by the inventor Clément Ader. Unorthodox, it looks like a giant bat. The aircraft hangs from the ceiling at the apex of a cavernous marble stairwell and can be viewed from above or below. Christened "*Éole*" after the Greek god of winds, this was the first aircraft in the world to fly under its own power, lifting eight inches off the ground and travelling for a hundred and sixty feet. A modest journey, to be sure, but still an example of powered flight, predating the Wright Brothers by over a decade. Ader was obsessed with bats; he raised them in droves for his studies, adapting their organic aerodynamics into a template for *Éole*. His creation embodied the refinements of art, especially the great wings, constructed with bamboo rods to mimic the bones and covered with a skin of coarse fabric. The pilot sits in an oblong buggy suspended between the wings, just behind a light-weight steam engine invented by Ader to drive the propeller. Clunky yet beautiful, it casts a spell over the viewer—a sculpture that dreams of the air.

Science as vertigo seemed to be a key theme of the museum. After I developed a crick in my neck from gawking at the overhead marvel of *Éole,* I filed on like a zombie to the next dizzying opportunity. In the train room (and of course there's a train room), I watched a video projection of the electric TGV (*Train à Grand Vitesse)* setting a land speed record. Entirely for scientific purposes, they mounted a camera to capture the view from the cockpit at 500 km/hour. Susan and I love the French rail system, one of the best in the world, and we have lounged peacefully in a TGV zooming along the tracks at 300 km/hour. Such rapid transit allows the passenger, for a modest fee, to travel from Paris to Marseilles in three hours. I soon learned not to gaze out the window without a distant vista for focus, otherwise, the scenery rips past at an alarming clip. When I introduced my grown son to the delights of French trains, he got sick. The video of the land speed record rivaled the devil's own hypnotism. I couldn't take my eyes away from the screen, even though there was nothing to see but a smeared blur of trees. While captured by this peculiar eye torture, I thought *so that's what 500 km/hour looks like*. There might have been other thoughts, but they were obliterated in nausea. At the end of the video, as the train slowed down, the camera rotated around the cabin to take in the crew and a delegation of railroad officials along for the ride, first-hand witnesses to history. I'm sure it was a ride that no one wanted to stay in the office and miss. In a testament to the importance of *joie de vivre*, they were laughing and toasting each other with champagne. Perhaps they had been drinking the whole time, who would know?

Queasy, I staggered away from the video monitor before it could replay and looked for something stable. Susan had skipped the trains to check out other stuff, so I wandered off to find her: she was a reliable source of stability. I located her in the stairwell, back to contemplating *Éole* and with hundreds of photos to prove it. I commented that we'd surpassed our standard one-hour museum limit. We'd only seen a portion of the exhibits, but experience had convinced us that beyond the one-hour mark there's little to gain but brain blisters and sore feet.

We agreed to return to the museum another day, see the rest, and share the marvels with our friends, but we never did. There's always another compelling distraction in Paris. Because of this, we didn't see the place where Umberto Eco's protagonist stowed away, an unfortunate oversight. Ironically, he hid in a room devoted to the technology of glass. Within the novel, Eco forces his character to recite an inventory of the contents: "A jumble of a room, Chinese porcelain alongside androgynous vases of Lalique, potteries, majolica, faïence, and Murano, and in an enormous case in the rear, life-size and three-dimensional, a lion attacked by a serpent." According to Eco, whose descriptions of this museum are even more obsessive than my own, behind the glass sculpture of the lion and serpent there is a giant periscope. To look through the periscope, you step into an enclosed "sentry-box" and are exposed to a refracted, wide-angle view of the streets surrounding the museum. Eco's hero slipped into the box and decided that if found there by a guard, it'd be plausible to claim he was so mesmerized that he lost track of time. I think that's a credible excuse. Throughout the museum, the visitor encounters technology as a sequence of beguiling fetishes. Normally, our unconscious relationship with tools and machines avoids the light of day, taken for granted as a function of being human. Within the halls of this old priory, the veil is raised, and the secular, seductive magic is out in the open, polished to please every desire. Knowing this hardly dispels the fascination. In the end, I'm only sorry we missed the sentry box periscope. Chances are, if we had found it, we would still be there.

6

The Coin Purse in Theory and Practice [Ennis 2018]

In my thigh pocket I had eleven and eightpence in a weighty pendulum of mixed coins.

Flann O'Brien, *At-Swim-Two-Birds*

Don't even try to get through Europe without a coin purse. Hardly an affectation or display accessory, the purse provides a way to deal with the abundance of coined money. The smallest paper bill in the euro zone is the five euro note. As a result, the one and two-euro coins receive heavy circulation—and I do mean "heavy." Because many items are inexpensive and priced in fractions, you can't even avoid the sub-euro denominations: fifty cents, twenty, ten, five, two, and one, making a total of eight different coins you will need at one time or another. Don't expect these coins to have a logical gradation of size to value; when I open my coin purse, it's a jumble of confusion. I pick at the metal disks, never able to find what I need without a struggle that reminds me how stupid my fingers are. At least I have the purse, a soft leather pouch that sits with lumpy gravity in my pocket and opens its mouth with a grin when I peer inside. You could carry the coins loose in your pocket, as I did for a while, but I grew tired of coins leaping and dribbling through my fingers and onto the floor during the extraction process. It didn't take long to understand why coin purses were sold in markets and shops everywhere around the continent. As soon as I did the addition, I bought one.

My favorite purse, made in Corsica, slipped into the hand of a pickpocket on the Paris Metro, never to be seen again. Acceding to the common wisdom of women, I then purchased a small shoulder bag and used it to carry wallet, coin purse, passport, and other key items. I reserved my pocket for a tattered handkerchief, which no one stole, though they would have been welcome to it.

I toted the coin purse everywhere and had it with me one day as I walked into the post office of Ennis, County Clare, Ireland. I only ducked in to mail a birthday card to my son in the United States. I love him so much that I was prepared to pay a minor fortune. The friendly woman at the window stated a price far less than I expected, and I diverted my hand from its course toward the wallet and redirected it to the coin purse instead. I unzipped the purse and gazed inside, hoping that the proper coins would be on the top. This was not the case. I plunged into the usual fumble, drawing out a handful and staring at them in my open palm, trying to identify the ones I needed. It was embarrassing -- after a year in Europe I still had trouble differentiating the coinage.

The clerk interrupted my meditation. "You'll be wanting to get rid of the brown ones, now, won't you?"

I stared at her like a dimwit.

She smiled, brow arched and with a slight curl to her lips, conveying both gentle tolerance and incipient mirth. Reaching across the counter, she plucked a 5-cent coin from my palm and held it up. It was browner than the others. "Out with it," she said, tapping the countertop between us, "all of it."

Dutifully, I emptied the contents of the coin purse onto the counter. I watched in amazement as she sorted through the mess, retrieving all the 5-cent coins. These were abundant; I could never count the smaller denominations fast enough during retail transactions—generally I settled for handing over the easily identified one euro coins, a tactic that only generated more wayward money. She patiently assembled the amount required for the postage in 5-cent pieces, then pushed the rest back. No one, in any country, had ever shown me such an interesting kindness. I was pleased and thanked her profusely as I scraped the remaining coins into the purse.

"Ah yes," she said, "we took care of the brown ones now, didn't we?" She spoke as if our Irish/American collaboration had rid the world of a scourge. I left the post office happy, with a lighter coin purse, and a new appreciation for the value of small change in promoting international goodwill.

7

The Stones We Leave Behind
[Carnac 2017]

...a testament of the rocks from all the dead unto some the living.

James Joyce, *Finnegans Wake*

TERMS OF MEGALITHERY
Menhir: a single standing stone
Cromlech: a circle of menhirs
Dolmen: a capped dome assembled from stones, originally covered by earth as the core of a barrow mound

Did our ancestors really have nothing better to do than wrestle with titanic rocks and assemble puzzles in stone? Traveling the megalithic circuit of Western Europe, I couldn't shake that question. In all sorts of places, some quite surprising, rock structures dominate greenswards with the authority of gods or thrust from the forest floor like giant, crystallized mushrooms. Who built these things and why? They are very old; we know that much and not a lot more. Some structures feature astronomic alignments, a curiosity that galvanizes speculation about the motives of the ancients. Are they calendars marking the ritual progress of the seasons or are they landing beacons for alien spacecraft? Opinions proliferate with or without facts. For better or worse, the mystery has fueled an industry of imagination appealing to tourists, profiteers, fabulists, crackpots, archaeologists, and aspiring time travelers.

Susan and I can't get enough of these megalithic wonders. When we embarked for an extended stay in France, we prioritized a visit to Carnac on the Bretagne peninsula, the site of one of the most perplexing megalith constructions in all of Europe. Photographs I'd seen made it look like nothing else in the realm of prehistory. I'd wanted to go there for years. Plus, the area is famous for its buckwheat crêpes, and food is always a motivation.

Although the region is called Brittany by the British and Bretagne by the French, it is neither French nor British. The native Bretons—Celtic remnants—call it Breizh, and they have their own language and traditions, not to mention their own flag. Should you go there, they will gladly remind you about this. The quiet old village of Carnac is on the southern coast of the peninsula, overlooking sandy beaches and extensive oyster farms. Tourists come in the summer to lay on the sand, surf, eat, and marvel at the ancient stones.

Neolithic constructions are commonplace in the Breizh countryside, but at Carnac you encounter the climax of these efforts: the world's largest installation of standing stones. The central alignments range across four kilometers of fields and woods: eleven roughly parallel rows of menhirs that file over the undulating landscape like the backbones of dragons. They occupy the land with the authority of six thousand years. The menhirs vary in size from headstone scale to giants that rise nineteen feet in the air and weigh 77 tons. The rows meander slightly across the earth, giving the impression of something that grew rather than a building material dragged there and set carefully in place. Interpolated at various points into the rows are small cromlechs and dolmens. The menhirs display no consistent pattern incorporating size or shape. Big ones are next to little ones in random combinations, forming rows of haphazard line-ups. Four thousand stones have been cleared out of the brush, so far. More sleep forgotten in the dense vegetation of the woods.

Five minutes into wandering around the alignments and I remarked on what, for me, was the key feature of the installation: the broad sides of the menhirs all face south, reflecting the light of the coastal sun. They stand in lines across the earth, eleven deep and stretching over two miles, watching the sky like sentinels.

Each day we returned to the installation and explored different sections. The alignments have no center to draw the pedestrian, so we meandered through the grassy fields, traversing back and forth to appreciate the individual character of the upright stones. We admired and caressed their surfaces, adorned by lichens in shades of gray, green, black, and orange. Everywhere we rambled, I had the same impression of lithic patience, of waiting, of the freedom of stones to be still.

Of course, the subtle atmospherics of the megaliths have been distilled into the brash industries of tourism. In the village you can buy small plastic models of menhirs, incised with the *triskelion*, the three-legged spiral symbol marked on Neolithic stones, Celtic shields, illuminated manuscripts, and recently adopted as the symbol of a far-right Breton nationalist group. Or you may, for a fee, climb on an automotive caravan made to look like an amusement park mini-train, festooned with advertising, and wind your way around the nearby megalith sites at a torpid pace while traffic piles up behind. The caravan never stops, even to let cars go by, so you don't have to get out and mingle with the stones. The childish train left us more puzzled than the monuments. Why would anyone prefer such a vantage to inspect these amazing objects? The stones stand as they have for thousands of years; do they not deserve to be admired in like-minded stillness? As we took advantage of the numerous trails curling through the fields and woods, we met a few other solemn pedestrians, like pilgrims wandering among the stones. But mostly we had the monuments to ourselves. Our only concession to the annoying commercial culture was to purchase, at one of the local *patisseries*, a *baguette de menhir*, which, like all baguettes, had the appearance of an oblong rock, yet was crunchy and chewy and tasted like whole grain.

It was early fall, the off-season for Carnac. A few tourists rode the silly train and strolled through town looking for things to buy, but the locals had exhausted their interest in hustling souvenirs and stayed home with their families. Most shops were closed. It was even hard to find an open restaurant. With no retail distractions, we spent our week in Carnac roaming around the woods and fields. Unfortunately, once again I couldn't find a decent chart of the area and had to rely on the imprecise, advertisement-laden map from the tourist bureau. Never quite lost yet never oriented either, we managed to navigate our way to megaliths. Of course, they're everywhere; you can walk in any direction.

One day, after negotiating a confusing knot of trails in a dark forest, we found *Le Géant*, a solitary menhir. It stands twenty feet above the ground like a truncated redwood or the literal lithic phallus of a god. We worshipped by walking it in circles, trailing our hands across the rugged surface. It seemed a little precarious and despite its obvious sacred nature, I couldn't stop thinking profanely about the thing falling over on top of us.

We encountered cromlechs and dolmens here and there, in the alignments and scattered through the woods, but basically this was a realm of menhirs and most of the four thousand counted stones stood in the main rows. Meandering through this project and arriving at a high point, looking back and forth, we perceived no end to the stones marching across the earth like the legion of a faded empire. The labor required for the construction was incomprehensible, involving generations and several thousands of years. I imagined dedicated cohorts dragging new slabs and boulders to the alignments, slowly leveraging them into place amidst ceremonies long forgotten. It reminded me of how I'd helped a neighbor lay stone for a foundation to his cabin. The two of us excavated with shovels and carefully fitted together stones we'd gathered from the surrounding forest, somehow loading them into a pickup and driving slowly to the site, careful not to blow the compressed shocks. We used the biggest stones we could handle, moving them by rocking and revolving, like you would a refrigerator, even though none was larger than the size of a large suitcase. The foundation took a year to build and nearly wrecked my back. Even hefting and laying the smaller stones required labor beyond reason. Yet there's something inherently satisfying in building things with rocks. It feels like a gesture against time. There's a kind of hope in it, a faith of durability.

Our hosts in Carnac, Luc and Valerie, lived in a large home on the edge of town. They rented out the top floor apartment, curiously decorated in the style of Jules Verne's submarine in *Twenty Thousand Leagues Under the Sea*. After a day spent outdoors, hiking for miles under sun or storm, it provided a snug nest. Luc was born and raised two houses away on land that's been in the family for generations. When Valerie, from another village, married Luc, they built their present house as a team. Neither of them could speak more than a few words in English but they were energetic in extending their hospitality as representatives of Carnac and Breizh. They had little interest in Paris, and I don't think they considered themselves to be French, exactly. In truth, they loved their native land with a non-ideological passion. As history buffs, they hoped to start a tour guide business that focused, not on megaliths, but on the rich involvement of the area in World War II. For Luc and Valerie, Americans still represented the liberators, and our presence was regarded with favor. They relished the shared history of shooting Nazis, and one of their passions was caretaking the nearby cemetery for American war dead.

Luc enlisted me in his pet project. Three Black American soldiers had been killed in fighting around Carnac during the war, and their remains had never been identified. Luc and his fellow enthusiasts wanted to erect a monument to these men for the upcoming seventy-fifth anniversary, but they wanted the names. Since I was American, he asked that I contact the Army and get them. Touched by his gesture, I agreed, though I had to curb my skepticism. It seemed as likely as excavating the names of the people who erected the megaliths. Luc gave me the text of a military log describing the combat incident where the men were killed. It totaled about forty words, including coordinates. This was all he had, but I agreed to pursue the matter.

Being good hosts, Luc and Valerie humored our fascinations regarding prehistory. Urging us to see the megaliths at sunset, they pointed out a convenient shortcut from the house. We followed their suggestion and though the sun hid behind a cloudy Atlantic horizon, we had a sublime experience, just the two of us on a slow dance through the menhirs. We recognized the life in the stones, and in the dusky quiet, we felt it. Each stone conveys a unique character; when you touch the surface, it's like stroking the cheek of a craggy old woman or man, as if the ancestors hardened themselves to rock. They stand on the earth and bear witness, even if nobody remembers why.

Later, after returning to Paris, we watched an online video of a lecture by a British ex-pat who lives in Carnac. He claims to have solved the riddle of the alignments; a claim met with doubt by archaeologists. During his taped lecture, he broke down the engineering specifications of the structure, accompanying his analysis with power point schematics as endless and mysterious as the stones themselves. Periodically, he arrived at revelations such as "…and the angle is… [dramatic pause] …27.625 degrees."

This would be followed by a snickering giggle, as if to emphasize the inevitability of the geometry. Repeated calculations yielded the same result, accompanied by further triumphant snickers. We watched the entire video, speechless, stunned by the diligence of his mad obsession.

Scientists may forever be baffled by the Carnac alignments. I'm not sure I want to know any more than I do, which is that they are beautiful, and the stones watch the sky with ancient dedication. Maybe it's a natural product of the land and the people it breeds. I admired the dedication of Luc and Valerie, their interest in a meaningful legacy, their willingness to honor the sacrifice of others. Like their ancestors lost in time, they wanted to raise a monument in stone, a proclamation of human nobility. I made inquiries with the Army and the Red Cross, but nothing came of it. No matter, I'm sure Luc and Valerie set up their memorial, honoring the unknown soldiers. They'll pass their story on to the children and so forth, until it dissipates into the mist of centuries. Then, when all the signs are worn away, their stone will remain, among the others, another witness to the world.

8

Putting the Body Back Together [Crete & Naxos 2019]

If you take Greece apart, in the end you will see remaining to you an olive tree, a vineyard, and a ship. Which means: with just so much you can put her back together.

Odysseus Elytis, "The Little Seafarer," *Collected Poems*

We no longer believe in the myth of the existence of fragments that, like pieces of an antique statue, are merely waiting for the last one to be turned up, so that they may all be glued back together to create a unity that is precisely the same as the original unity.

Gilles Deleuze & Felix Guattari, *Anti-Oedipus: Capitalism and Schizophrenia*

As soon as I could read on my own, I devoured any and all children's books rehashing the Greek myths, lingering over the illustrations of swords, heroes, and monsters. Starting in the elementary school library and progressing to the public, I ransacked the shelves like a barbarian. I read the books and I saw the movies. Certainly, I would have seen Kirk Douglas in the 1954 spectacle "Ulysses," because Douglas was one of my mother's favorite actors and we saw everything he did whether it was age-appropriate or not. Kirk did a great job mugging and flexing his brawn among the overdubbed and underdressed Italian cast. The film industry continued in that vein, churning out mythic sensations irresistible to a boy: "Jason and the Argonauts," "Helen of Troy," "Minotaur: The Wild Beast of Crete," even "The Three Stooges Meet Hercules." Saturated with the imagery and narrative of these fables, I couldn't get enough, and my lifelong appetite for fantasy should be blamed on Greek mythology.

Like snow melting out of the mountains and finding its way to the lowlands, the Greek myths percolated into our culture, occupying spaces in the bedrock, and serving as a fundamental wellspring of inspiration. Traces of this body of work are inescapable, from athletes echoing the boasts of old heroes to psychologists wrangling metaphors of the unconscious. Last year, another English translation of Homer was published, to great acclaim. No matter how old and removed, the material still speaks. Yet in Greece, as I learned, there is more to it. The myths are not just a heritage of the past: they live on, in the stories people tell and in the gods you meet.

When my wife, Susan, and I arrived on the island of Naxos, one of our hosts, learning that we had just come from Crete, launched into the myth of Ariadne. Nikitas told us how Theseus, an elitist cad from Athens, seduced the beautiful Minoan princess, used her to vanquish the Minotaur, then off-loaded her on Naxos before he returned home. She'd outlived her utility; besides, he knew his father wouldn't approve of the match. Ariadne survived the rejection and, as consolation, mated with the god Dionysos and founded a lineage on Naxos. While driving us from the ferry, Nikitas told this story as if he himself had picked Ariadne up at the dock just last week. He went on: "Crete and Naxos are more alike than any other islands in the Aegean." Thus, the journey taken by Ariadne affirmed our own itinerary, at least in the eyes of Nikitas. But we'd already made the connection. When Susan suggested we go to Naxos as well as Crete, she wanted to follow the footsteps of the visionary food writer Patience Gray, former island resident, and author of the classic guide to Mediterranean cooking, *Honey from A Weed*. I quickly agreed because I'd heard the tale of Ariadne long before Nikitas told it and had always wanted to retrace the route, gathering up her threads.

Before Naxos, we spent two weeks in Crete, mostly exploring the northwestern shore around the port of Chania, a three-thousand-year-old city of fascinating complexity. Out of curiosity to see the southern, wilder side of the island and wade in the Libyan Sea, we bought bus tickets to the famous beach of Elafonisi. Over two hours each way, the route twisted through mountains and gorges. Erosion, especially in the gorges, chewed away at the road, dragging the outside lane into the abyss, and cluttering the remaining tarmac with boulders from above. Our driver, a buff young man with stubble and wrap-around sunglasses, was proud of his chariot, a new, full-size Mercedes-Benz bus. He approached driving as if he were on the battle fields of Troy, swerving and dodging every obstacle like our lives depended on it, as indeed they did. Where the road narrowed to a single lane, he hardened into Achilles and bore down on any offending traffic, forcing them to back around corners or take the ditch. He didn't flinch at goats or sheep wandering into the road, and we heard the livestock scurry to the side in a clatter of bells.

By the time the bus pulled into a gravel parking lot, we were keen to get out and put our feet back on the ground. My research had found trails to walk at either end of the beach. What I hadn't reckoned on was the heat. The sun of Helios hammered down on the coast as it traversed the sky, rendering the shoreline into an anvil of radiation, even in October. As far as we could see, there was no shade to darken the endless shore of rocks, sand, and scrub. Hiking here required full desert preparation instead of our ill-conceived quart of water and a couple of apples. Cowed by the prospects of wandering far, we trooped down to the beach. Many folks have rated it as one of the best in the world, though I couldn't imagine why. A hundred yards offshore, the water was still only ankle deep. The sand burned our feet, so we spent most of the time curled up in the shade of our rented sunbed (ten euros for the day). When we had to pee, it cost a euro to use the vile elevated outhouse, with no charge for the stench. After we'd gobbled our apples, we forced ourselves to approach the rustic food kiosk, where we inspected the choices of greasy hamburger-like objects and ice cream. We spent another ten euros on miniature ice cream bars.

The bus traveled to the beach, sat for five hours, then returned to Chania. That's what you got for the price of your ticket. We were warned that if we weren't back on the bus in time, it would leave anyway, and we would spend the night at Elafonisi. Given the choice of frolicking in the tepid foot baths of the Libyan Sea, subsisting on over-priced desserts, or burning to death in the sun, we were highly motivated to be back on the bus.

We marked our time on the shore like Odysseus did on the island of Calypso, lounging in the idyll but chafing to be away. Despite the generally undesirable nature of the place, at least to my taste, people kept showing up, hundreds and hundreds of them. They seemed to either stand in the water and display skin or sit and gaze at the others. Most people seemed to be enjoying themselves. I wouldn't say it was horrible; if you had shade, you were likely to survive. At some point we observed the driver strutting through the sand in his trunks, towel in one hand and sunscreen in the other, channeling the demeanor of a Greek god, and ignoring the looks of the tourists who couldn't help but admire his well-oiled passage.

On the way to Elafonisi, Susan commented that he was a good driver. Probably true, but we had sat in the back of the bus and couldn't see much of the action. During the return trip, we made the mistake of sitting near the front and every sharp turn with a five-hundred-foot drop looked like the end. At one point, as the driver swung the bus around a precipitous corner without slowing down, Susan yelled, "Jesus Christ!" The driver didn't flinch or look up. He might even have given it a little more gas. Who dares to second guess the gods?

In the beginning, according to the oldest Greek creation story, a goddess danced out of chaos. As an adolescent, I imagined this scene in my own version of a Hollywood spectacle. I'd seen the art history books and inspected the erotic details of Greek vase paintings. After my studies, I knew exactly what the goddess of creation looked like: voluptuous yet lithe, draped in flimsy garments, hair flowing down her back, wild and free. If I hadn't already left behind the Protestantism of my parents, I would have abandoned it in a second to worship such a being. To my mind, the Greeks had a much clearer idea of religion.

Inspired by her own beauty, the dancing goddess wanted something more substantial for a stage than ethereal chaos, so she divided sea from sky and whirled off in a tangle of hair. Come to think of it, since it was the origin of the world and pre-dated the fashion industry, she might have been naked, cloaked only in her hair. Of course, as those wavy locks whipped and spiraled around her figure, much was revealed. Or would have been if there was anyone to witness. As she moved, she generated winds that curled and tickled her skin. On impulse, she grabbed strands of air and wove them into a mighty serpent. Thrilled at coming into being, the snake preened and bobbed along with the goddess. Before long, he filled his slinky body with lust and they coupled on the waves, shivering in excitement between the ocean and the sky.

> *The retinue [of Dionysos] is composed of female maenads and most emphatically male satyrs. The maenads, who are always clothed, often with a fawn-skin over the shoulder, dance in a trance, with heads bowed or thrown far back. The appearance of the satyrs with their mixture of human and animal features is to be understood as a form of masking: a flat-nosed face mask with a beard and animal ears conceals the identity of the wearer, and a loin cloth holds the very often erect leather phallos and the horse tail. ... The significance of the phallos is not procreative... It is arousal for its own sake...*
>
> Walter Burkert, *Greek Religion*

We walked through the tourist section of Naxos Town along a boulevard of souvenir shops jammed between restaurants. I grew tired of looking at tee shirts and ball caps emblazoned with whatever shit someone thought would sell. Then I noticed an outdoor rack of cooking aprons. The apron at the front of the display offered the life-size image of a naked male torso with washboard abs and a pendulous organ. I would have been shocked, thinking of how many local children run up and down the street, but we'd been in Greece for a couple of weeks already and it was unremarkable. The museums proudly display the cultural heritage, highlighted by every sort of nudity, and I suppose that after a few thousand years of seeing these things it becomes commonplace.

Getting back to the creation story, though, the serpent phallos was not only aroused, it was also potent. The goddess soon expanded with new life, took the form of a dove, and brooded on the surface of the sea. Then she laid an egg. She gave the egg to the serpent and instructed him to coil around it seven times, at which point it split open, spilling out the contents of the universe as we now know it: sun, moon, stars, mountains, trees, rivers, lizards, herbs—everything, including a lot of rocks.

The doting goddess and her consort settled in on Mount Olympus and surveyed the wonders of their new realm. The snake, being a snake, soon proclaimed himself to be the sole creator of this universe, a boast that turned heads in public and, in time, made its way back to the goddess. She harbored no patience for serpentine lies and stomped his head flat, kicked out his teeth, and threw the vile thing into the bowels of the earth, where he and his kind remain.

In my youth, this story not only appealed to the imagination, but it also confirmed everything I suspected about life. My own snake promised no end of trouble and embarrassment. And it was clear that despite all the bragging and posturing of men, women made the important decisions. At least that was true in our house. My mother ran it, top to bottom. Men may have worked hard to stuff women back into the chaos where they came from, but even Zeus couldn't get away with that.

There is a kind of flame in Crete—let us call it 'soul'—something more powerful than either life or death. There is pride, obstinacy, valor, and together with these something else inexpressible and imponderable, something which makes you rejoice that you are a human being, and at the same time tremble.

Nikos Kazantzakis, *Report to Greco*

On our first day of walking around the intricate passages of Chania, in Crete, we were fascinated by the graffiti art climbing up, down, and across the walls. Most of it was written in Greek, of course; I couldn't read the letters, let alone the words. But the imagery was clear, and the occasional English left no doubt; everywhere we looked we saw the same proclamation: "no fascism." Posters and every other form of street media reiterated this sentiment; Chania seemed a treacherous place to be a fascist.

We found a health food store and walked in, always interested in how these businesses manifest in other cultures. A young woman sat behind the counter reading a book. She nodded as we entered, offered the standard greeting "ya sas" ("your health"), and went back to her book. We inspected the contents of the store, noting that it looked like a typical American health food store. In the back corner, I found a tee shirt hanging on the wall. Black, with a red and gray logo, it appeared to offer a working-class theme, but I couldn't interpret the image and I certainly couldn't understand the Greek. However, from a graphic perspective, it was cool, and of course, I wanted it.

I approached the young woman and asked if she spoke English. She carefully put down her book, marked her spot, and said "yes." I asked if she could explain the meaning of the shirt.

I followed her to the back of the store where she studied the design as if seeing it for the first time. She touched the inscription with her finger, lost in thought. "It is a metaphor," she said. "I don't know how to say it. Working together--makes the wheel go round. Something like that. Do you understand?"

"I think so. Solidarity... or collective action... owning the means of production...."

"Something like that," she said.

I told her I would buy the shirt and we returned to the register. As she rang the transaction, I ventured another question. "Is there a lot of antifascist feeling here?"

She smiled. "You noticed?"

"Oh yes."

"Good! If a visitor can tell, that is good!" She went on with pride to explain that Crete has expelled all fascist organizations. Recently, popular resistance had forced the Golden Dawn, an ultra-right group, to close its office and leave the island. Crete, she assured me, was the most left-wing region of Greece. I didn't doubt it. Then she asked about Bernie Sanders. When I told her that he had just had a heart attack, she looked mortified. "I did not know," she said grimly, as if it was her own relative.

"Please come back while you are here," she said as we left.

Two weeks later found us in Heraklion, Crete's largest city. It's also called Irakleio, since the Greeks, like the Irish, apply multiple spellings for every name. Susan's research uncovered a restaurant not far from our hotel that had a reputation for good food and leftist politics; impossible to pass up.

After a stroll through narrow streets abloom with murals and arbor-cooled outdoor cafes, we arrived at the destination: the

Café of Kagiampi. There were a few tables on the sidewalk, so we sat in the one closest to the door and waved at the proprietor through the open wall. Like most restaurants in Greece, outside and inside occupy continuous space. The walls inside the café were crammed from floor to ceiling with framed portraits of Greek radicals, hundreds of them, like heroes in a pantheon. In the rear, a large Cuban flag hung over the counter and behind it a woman cooked in an unhurried manner. A trim, elderly man, presumably Kagiampi himself, set our table; when he discovered we didn't speak Greek, he walked away and sent the cook to take our order. Her recitation of the specials was difficult for us to understand but her good humor and warmth made it clear that none of this mattered. I ordered a dish of traditional Cretan grain with mixed vegetables, while Susan opted for pork in wine sauce.

We shared our food, and I thought Susan's dish was the most delicious serving of pork I have ever tasted. The grain, which the cook claimed was an ancient variety, reminded me of quinoa. We stuffed ourselves and sat back with satisfaction, watching pedestrians, and sipping mineral water. The proprietor brought over a chair and sat down with us. He thumped a massive book on the table. "Where are you from?" he asked in broken English.

"The evil empire," I replied.

He looked at me blankly. "Where?"

"The United States," I confessed.

His eyes lit up. "America! We like America!" He tapped a finger on the book. "Once America had largest Communist Party in the world. History!" He put the book in my hands. I thumbed through it; of course, it was in Greek, which might as well have been Tibetan. With some effort, I was made to understand that the book was a history of the US Communist Party before World War II. Kagiampi treasured the book because he wanted to understand what went wrong in America, that such a great movement disappeared.

The conversation quickly mired in linguistic problems and Kagiampi recruited the young, long-haired man at the next table to translate. This fellow turned from his female companion and gladly joined our project. He confirmed that Kagiampi wanted to know what happened to America. They all did, really, the Greeks. I wanted to say that Stalin soured a lot of Americans on Communism but thought better of opening such complexities. Instead, I took a more hopeful tack and pointed out that socialism was no longer an impossible word in American politics. The translator asked, "You mean Bernie Sanders?" In Crete, they all wanted to know about Sanders.

"Yes," I said, "but also on local levels, socialists are winning a few seats in government."

We all nodded in unison, satisfied with even meager political progress.

Kagiampi picked up his book and stood. "I study history," he said.

We shook hands.

As in all Greek restaurants, once you sit at a table, you may live there. If you want to pay your bill, you have to ask for it. After paying, I was instructed to return to the table so that we could be served a plate of fruit and a honey-saturated cake along with a flask of raki and two shot glasses, on the house. Sharing raki is a point of pride in Crete. We had to say twice that we didn't drink alcohol. I worried that we might seem rude, but our refusal, once understood, was tolerated with a smile.

We were only in Heraklion for two days, but we returned to Kagiampi's the next day to partake of more food and solidarity. Now we were comrades in the myth.

Transgression of boundaries is a recurrent theme in Greek mythology. The origin story of the Olympian gods provides a cascade of fornication, cannibalism, and murder. Sons impregnate their mothers and sisters and hang around to eat the children as they enter the world. At the beginning of this unruly saga, Mother Earth emerged from chaos; she birthed gods, titans, and other creatures, most of whom didn't play well together. After two generations of mayhem, Zeus was born to Rhea, who was his aunt as well as his mother. Because Cronus, his titan father, wanted little Zeus for a snack, Rhea begged her mother to spirit him away to a remote cave in Crete. Mother Earth obliged her daughter, but couldn't stay, since her presence on Olympus was a necessary component of the family drama. Instead, two nymphs cared for baby Zeus, raising him on honey and goat milk. Later, after growing up, he killed his father and became Lord of the Universe. He rewarded his nurse, the goat, by elevating her into the heavens as Capricorn. And in generosity to the nymphs, Zeus gave them one of the goat's horns, the Cornucopia or horn of plenty, so that they would never run out of food and drink. The Cretans have so much gratitude for this cornucopia that they will show you, with pride, the exact cave where Zeus was raised. Of course, being Greek, they disagree about which cave is the right one.

Every Saturday in Chania, a side street of the old town is occupied by hundreds of farmers hawking produce. The variety and heartiness of the fruits, vegetables, herbs, and cheeses proves that Zeus' cornucopia still yields a bounty. The street is narrow and both sides are lined with stalls and goods jammed so close together that often I couldn't tell where one ended and the next one began. While Susan stuffed a bag with spinach the size of palm fronds, I watched as two feet away a stout, grizzled vendor wrapped his hand around three walnuts and crushed them. He opened a heroic fist to offer perfectly cracked nuts to a woman already struggling with full shopping bags. The three of us were nearly shoulder to shoulder in that casual Greek way of defining physical space. The woman smiled and admired the nuts while they chatted in rapid fire Greek. The dialogue was friendly and lasted for several minutes, but no nuts exchanged hands. I wanted to try a walnut myself, they looked so good, or even test my ability to crack them in my bare hand, but I remained mute and passive. Being a tourist, nothing was expected of me anyway.

We bought large bags of dark, ratty-looking oranges so that we could drink fresh-squeezed juice every morning. Such oranges would never be sold over a counter in the United States due to their mottled appearance, but they were hand grenades of flavor. All the produce in Crete tasted divine and we ate like gods. Tomatoes, feta or graviera cheese, cucumbers, spinach, toast, all sliced and smothered in olive oil—this became our principal meal. I learned that Cretans consume, on average, over three times as much olive oil as Italians or Spaniards. They even use it in desserts and pastries. It's a rare restaurant that doesn't serve a bottle of oil along with the meal, in case the food isn't saturated to your standards. The so-called Mediterranean diet was originally based on studies of Cretan peasants, who outlive everyone else in southern Europe. Nutrition researchers identify the olive as a principal agent in this longevity. Olive trees grow in all the available nooks and crannies and are revered as the tree of life. A tree of three thousand years is enshrined near Kalymbari with its own courtyard and museum. Every four years a few sprigs are harvested to make a wreath for the winner of the Olympic marathon.

Having sampled from this cornucopia, I'm a believer.

Pursuing further delights for our taste buds in Chania, Susan's internet research discovered a vegetarian restaurant. It was famous for its spinach pies, a favorite food of mine. After wandering around the stone wharfs of the old Venetian port, we found it on a side street. Even when you're standing in front of it, identifying a place can be a challenge due to the language. Of course, everything is signed in the Greek alphabet. I love the look of the letters and although I tried to decipher them, both cursive and capital, I struggled. But what can you expect from an alphabet designed by a god (Hermes) to resemble the flight patterns of his favorite birds (cranes)? Additionally, many signs offer Greek words in the Latin alphabet, an approximation that lends itself to a variety of spellings not always similar. Places that deal with tourists, such as restaurants and museums, often provide English, a feature that helped us more than once. On a large sign, the vegetarian restaurant declared "SLOW FOOD," which was how we knew we were at the right place. Excited for a new food adventure, we sat at a sidewalk table.

"Oh, your necklace! Is it a bee?" The young waitress beamed when she saw Susan's pendant. Susan nodded and we all admired the large, metallic bee before dealing with the business of menus, specials, and table setting. I thought how wonderful it was that such a fuss would be made over the pendant. In Crete, bees are holy creatures and apiculture can be traced back to Minoan times nearly four thousand years ago. Not only Zeus had been nourished by honey, but generations of subsequent mortals.

Stelios, a soft-spoken gnome of a chef, came to take our order, while the waitress, perhaps his daughter, tended to new arrivals. Stelios was a round man with a studied, deliberate style of moving and talking. His presence was soothing, and I wanted him to stay with us. Unnecessary, as we soon discovered, because a dining experience at his restaurant required a minimum of two hours and we would get to see plenty of him. The sign said slow food and it did not lie. The view from the sidewalk encompassed the elegant plane trees and palms in the park across the street, the sturdy Venetian fortress walls, and the sea beyond. Not a venue for fast food, anyway. I ordered a spinach pie and Susan ordered the special "Stelios' salad."

"And that must be you," she commented.

He bowed in acknowledgment. "If it is my salad, I should be in the kitchen making it," he joked.

An hour later, the salad, a masterpiece of fresh, wild greens, was delivered to the table. By that point, we had drifted into a trance, watching people, and letting the sea breeze caress our stray hairs. The table was our new home, and it was a fine place, indeed. The crust on the spinach pie had been made from a hearty, whole grain filo and I drowned it with additional olive oil. Given the chance, I was certain that I could live on this pie.

I paid the bill and returned to the table. A plate of apple slices, grapes, pomegranate seeds and a moist cake the waitress called "halva" appeared for the coup de grace. It sat in a puddle of dark honey. We lingered for another half an hour. And we came back at least two more times, taking refuge there once during a heavy rain shower. Stelios and his crew packed in as many soaked refugees as they could and tended to us all like visiting dignitaries. You can say it's just a business but eating at To Stachi Slow Food felt a lot more like going to church than any church I'd seen.

...it is the dancing leaps of the youths themselves in which this power of the god is present. ...the experience of the dance merges with the experience of the deity.

Walter Burkert, *Greek Religion*

The port of Chania circumscribes a harbor of perfect beauty, replicated on thousands of refrigerator magnets sold in every nook and cranny of the city. Built when Venice ruled the island five hundred years ago, the harbor forms an oval enclosure protected by high sea walls and capped with a lighthouse at the narrow entrance. Only the lower section of the original lighthouse remains. After the Turkish conquest in the seventeenth century, the new regime rebuilt the upper two thirds in the form of a minaret. Despite the overlapping styles, it's a graceful spire.

The inner shore of the port consists of expansive stone wharfs and plazas. A domed mosque stands in the middle of the large, central plaza. The Ottoman Empire ended over a hundred years ago and now the mosque functions as a multipurpose community center. The Cretans have no love for the Turks, who ruled Crete for three hundred years. Every town commemorates at least one plane tree where resistors were hung as a warning. Of course, these warnings provided fuel for the resistance. A fierce rebel spirit dwells in Crete, as in Ireland and Corsica, and multigenerational bitterness toward oppressors contributes to the working definition of honor. Perhaps as a symbol of retribution, or just as a practical matter, the mosque is an empty shell, stripped of all religious trappings inside and out.

One day, eagle-eyed Susan spotted a poster promoting an event in the plaza, right next to the mosque. The illustration showed two men distilling grape mash into raki, the national beverage and festivity propellant. There was enough English on the poster for us to understand that along with the raki, there would be traditional music and dance. Scheduled for the same evening, we knew we had to go, although most of the time we're too tired to venture out at night.

In the dusky dark, the port was alive with lights and people. Outdoor beams illuminated the walls of the lighthouse, and it resembled a glowing candle on the edge of the sea. We climbed the steps into the mosque; the door stood open, and we were curious. A musty odor permeated the barren interior. Two artists, a jeweler and a painter, both women, had covered the floor and walls with their art. We browsed with the discomfort of being the only customers and thus responsible for the well-being of the artists. Susan bought a pair of earrings while I inspected the abstract paintings. Suddenly, amplified Greek music pounded through the back wall from the plaza, resonating into the echo chamber of the mosque. The painter broke into a jig and announced, "Now we dance."

Singing and dancing in public makes me wary; I have little aptitude for either and hesitate to embarrass myself. However, the music pouring into the mosque was infectious. We rushed outside, leaving the artists to their lonely wares, and circled the building to join a crowd of hundreds arced around the back of the mosque. There, on a makeshift stage, bobbed a line of dancers dressed in traditional Cretan fashion. Behind them were three musicians, two men playing a guitar-like instrument known as a *laouto*, and one man singing while playing a *lyra*. The energy coming from these three modest instruments was intoxicating: hard-driving, wild, and free. The *lyra* player raced his bow across the three strings, creating a buzzing tone like a flight of bumblebees. The *laoutos* embellished the basic line, plucking and weaving it into a larger pattern, an encouragement to move, an invitation to dance. The ancient beauty of the music immediately took possession of my body and I twitched and bounced in place. I noticed Susan did the same. It seemed impossible to stay still, as if we had surrendered to the gods. It didn't surprise me to learn in the myths that the large stones for the walls of Thebes were moved solely by the magic of the *lyra*, for this instrument demands kinetic obedience.

As we opened our hearts to the music, our eyes feasted on the dancers. Hands linked to shoulders, they danced side by side, men and women, a circular dance flattened to a line to fit on the stage. At first stately and measured, the tempo accelerated, pushing the steps, simple at first yet growing more complex as I watched. At the left end, a man demonstrated the elevated leaps of the male component of the *pentozali*. He used the linking hand of the dancer next in line for stability and support, first executing an increasingly intricate jig, then jumping as high as he could, turning his body sideways, twisting his torso so he could slap boots and thighs in ritual precision on the way down. Depending on the dancer's athleticism, these maneuvers often evoked spontaneous cheers and applause. We even saw two men, one a boy, perform a standing flip while grasping the partner's hand. My wrist ached in sympathy.

Following the men's display, a woman broke from the line and skipped forward, arms elevated in the same pose shown on the Minoan frescoes painted over three thousand years ago, spinning, jigging, a dance of no less energy, with formidable grace and movement. Back and forth, individuals shared the limelight for a few minutes, then the men moved forward in a group, connected arm to arm, stomping and springing, the hard steps of a man's body. One source identified this dance as a relic of revolution, a celebration from the eighteenth century when the decision was made to rebel against the Turks. But that's not when it started. The basic moves date back to Minoan times, when the Cretans ruled the Aegean and if there was to be rebellion, and there always is, it would be against them. Regardless, the martial vigor is undeniable. When the men finished pounding their heavy boots on the stage, they fell back and the women advanced as a group, arms up, fingers touching, bouncing and spinning with another display of controlled abandon. The dance was never rigid; it remained unpolished and fluid with room for improvisation, yet always synchronous with the music.

Fascinated with every aspect of the performance, I studied the dancing costumes. The men dressed in a garb of short, baggy pantaloons, vests, sashes, and tall boots. A Cretan knife was stuffed into the sash and a black scarf wrapped around their heads. The fringe of the scarf hung in the eyes as symbols of grieving tears. The women wore long skirts with decorated panels, sashes, white blouses, and velvet vests embroidered with intricate, colorful designs. The vests clung with a similar cut as the bodices of Minoan times. In the old days the garment scooped low enough to display bare breasts, a style no longer in evidence at family events.

Troupe after troupe of dancers ascended the stage, cut loose for fifteen minutes, then filed off to let the next group continue the celebration. Many of these troupes were young, featuring children of elementary school age, all of whom could perform the dances with gusto and dignity. Twenty-four-hundred years ago, Euripides wrote "...the god has made no distinction between young and old, in calling them to the dance."

We watched in awe. I didn't see how anyone could stay still. In front of the stage, a four-year-old boy leaped and stomped, doing his best imitation of the men's dance, and when the women were in front, he danced along with them, too. Groups of ten or twenty danced at a time, expressing a collective body. Individual acrobatics and grace stood out but were quickly subsumed in the group. The energy belonged to the community and a tradition thousands of years old. Like many Americans, I have no personal connection to such a thing, this heritage of ancient tradition, and I've sensed its lack as an ache and an emptiness. Yet standing on the old stones of the plaza, as my muscles kept time to the rhythms, I wept. For a spell, I believed that I, too, belonged here and now: these were my people, this was my home. Such was the power of the art.

After an hour and a half of what could only be called a religious experience, there was a break and we wandered home, Susan dancing on my arm as we picked our way through the crowd and the soft night.

My principal anguish and the source of all my joys and sorrows from my youth onward has been the incessant, merciless battle between the spirit and the flesh.

Nikos Kazantzakis, *The Last Temptation of Christ* (prologue)

Orpheus, the magician of words and music, despite his longevity as a romantic symbol, was more of a sad sack than a hero. He botched his most famous deed (winning his girlfriend back from Hades), being too self-centered to follow a simple instruction. All he had to do was wait until she emerged into the light as she walked along behind him. But no, he turned to look at her as soon as the sun touched *his* face. Eurydice, dutifully following the sound of his lyre, was still in the shade, and there she remained. Some consider Orpheus' error a sign of ardor and eagerness, which is no doubt how he told it, yet it's a typical narcissistic blunder.

After tagging along with Jason and the Argonaut gang while they peddled mayhem around the Black Sea, Orpheus opted for a career change and started a cult. He cooked up an alchemical creation story and preached it with all the persuasion of his silver tongue. The Orphic story opened with the usual chaos divulging a goddess, in this case Night. She promptly fornicated with the wind (we're not told how) and laid an egg (silver, of course) in the womb of darkness (which sounds like her own womb, which would go without saying). The egg hatched and Eros popped out. This was not your valentine card Eros; this was an old-world god. The body featured both male and female sex, and they flew around on wings of gold, roaring, hissing, and bleating from the four heads mounted on their neck: a bull, a lion, a snake, and a ram. This barnyard personality bellowed everything into existence—earth, sky, sun, mountains, cats, dogs, and so on—thus establishing the universe as we know it.

Orpheus crooned his magic and lured recruits to the cult. Like many religious fanatics, he preferred asceticism and misogyny over biological distractions. He insisted on a vegetarian diet and, for god's sake if one had to have sex, it should be homosexual. Wine and meat were forbidden. As a partisan of chaste, sunny Apollo, he repeatedly offended Dionysos, the god of all those festivities that required wine, meat, and liberal sex. Orpheus was persuasive and charismatic, so eventually Dionysos had his maenads tear him to pieces, which was the end of his mortal coil, although there's a story that his head floated out to sea and washed up on the isle of Lesbos, still singing.

Before his end, though, Orpheus made a lasting contribution to human theology and philosophy. He proposed that the soul exists apart from the body and is immortal by nature. In earlier times, the Greeks failed to distinguish between matters of spirit and flesh—it was all one. But after Orpheus, a schism tore apart the phenomenon of human existence. Pythagoras and Plato elaborated the idea, as did Jesus and a legion of subsequent prophets and philosophers, and ever since we've been forced to reconcile living in two realms.

These are our native gods, the true ones, the immortals. Beneath such a sun, before such a sea, among such mountains, how could other gods—without bellies, without joy, without vine-leaves at their temples—have been born, how could they have thrived? And how could the sons and daughters of Greece have believed in a paradise different from this earthly paradise?

Nikos Kazantzakis, *Report to Greco*

Many years ago, when I planted trees in the forests of the Pacific Northwest, I worked with a guy who was a poet and a bit of a mystic, categories I included among my own aspirations. No one else on the crew discussed literature, so we became friends. He raved over a Greek writer, Nikos Kazantzakis, claiming that the guy understood everything important and captured all that in his writing. My friend loaned me a couple of books, including *The Last Temptation of Christ*, a novel banned by the Catholic Church—reason enough to read it. So far encouraged, I embarked on Kazantzakis' monumental work *The Odyssey: A Modern Sequel*, an epic poem narrating the second half of the life of Odysseus, picking up where Homer left off. Reading this tome was like manning the oars with the long-suffering hero through the seven seas of possibility—exhilarating yet exhausting. After that I put Kazantzakis down for many years.

In preparation for our trip to Greece, I picked him up again, reading *Zorba the Greek*. I'd seen the movie when it was released in 1964, but I figured the book would be a better place to dive into the culture. For our travels, I brought both volumes of Graves' *The Greek Myths* and planned to study mythology; I cast that boring notion aside as soon as we walked into a bookstore in Chania that offered novels in English. A fat one by Kazantzakis called *Freedom and Death* caught my attention. The blurb promised a novel about the last campaign of the Cretan revolution against the Turks. It was so good that as soon as I finished it, I went back to the bookstore for more. Eagerly, I selected an even bigger book by Kazantzakis, *Report to Greco*, his last work, an autobiographical novel.

I'd just started reading *Greco* when we arrived in Heraklion, the capital of Crete, and the port where we would catch the ferry to Naxos. After touring the Archaeological Museum, a facility stuffed to the brim with the treasures of Minoan civilization, we wandered around the passages of the old town. Susan found an antique store with a set of prayer beads that she wanted as a fidget for times of worry. While she paid the shopkeeper, I noticed that one wall of books, all in Greek, consisted entirely of works by Kazantzakis: older editions without dust jackets, shelf after shelf. By that time, I had learned to read most of the Greek alphabet and, given enough time, could work out a few words. In front of me, I contemplated an entire shelf of *The Odyssey*. Knowing what they were, and not knowing how to read them, left me frustrated with my ignorance.

"Susan, look at all these books by Kazantzakis!"

The owner perked up immediately. "You know Kazantzakis?"

"Oh yes. I read him. In English, but I read him. A great writer."

The owner nodded as if I had just said that the earth was under foot and the moon in the sky or some other indisputable fact. "I collect him. He is…" I never found out what he wanted to say because his English failed him. But I knew what he meant. Once Kazantzakis gets inside your blood, he takes over. Just that morning we had toured the Kazantzakis Museum, a tribute from the city where he grew up and is buried. The man is honored as an embodiment of the Greek passion for freedom. The owner motioned me over to his desk and rummaged in a drawer. He pulled out an old, battered box, the kind that have cushions inside to hold jewelry. He opened it and gently lifted out a pocket watch.

"This was his," he said.

I admire writers, thinkers, and artists, but I am most attached to the artifacts of their creativity, their books, paintings, or whatever they choose for public expression. The mundane elements of their lives are interesting to see, sometimes, and I'd been fascinated a few years ago to see the battered typewriter of one of my favorite writers. But an old pocket watch is really just an old pocket watch. The shop owner handled it like a holy relic. I wasn't sure if I should reach out to touch it, admire it at the distance, offer him a large amount of cash, or just fall to my knees. I settled for nodding my head and repeating myself. "A great writer," I said.

We rode to Naxos on one of the gigantic, high-speed catamarans that ply the waters of the Aegean, slicing across the sea at forty miles an hour. In Naxos Town, we settled into our spacious apartment, tired after the day of traveling and making connections, especially after an unscheduled layover amongst the tourist throngs on Santorini. That night I lay back on the bed to read before sleep and as I opened *Report to Greco*, I read about Kazantzakis and his family fleeing to Naxos from Heraklion. His nineteenth century steamship followed the same route as our catamaran, at a slower pace, no doubt, and without the distractions of television screens, arcade games, and other amenities for the modern sea traveler. Perhaps they spent the time reading or watching their native land fade into the horizon. Once the Kazantzakis family was safe, his father returned to Crete to fight against the Turks, helping to win freedom for the island.

The upper half of the central hill of Naxos Town is occupied by a labyrinthine Venetian fortress. In this part of the world, every town has its own archaeological museum, and this one, renowned for its Cycladic figurines, sits in the middle of the fort, at the summit of the hill. The museum used to be a Catholic school where the refugee Kazantzakis achieved scholastic note and was recruited for the Vatican, only to be rescued at the last minute by his Orthodox father, fresh from victory in Crete.

Three routes meander through the fortress to the summit. On the one we chose for the ascent, halfway up we came to a street marker identifying the passage as the way of "Nikos Kazantzakis." I took a picture of Susan standing in front of the sign, then we continued to huff and puff up the hill. When we arrived at the museum, I noted a Kazantzakis plaque affixed to the exterior, advertising his attendance at the former school. At this point, we had encountered so many traces of the man that he might as well have been sleeping in our bed.

On our last night in Naxos, as part of a culture festival, there was a showing of "Zorba the Greek." Susan had never seen the movie and we were charmed with the idea of viewing it in Greece, so we went, even though it required another ascent of the fortress. Arriving at the old monastery hall, we paid to sit on folding chairs and sipped complementary water, declining the offer of free raki. The film was shown in the original English (with Greek subtitles), but the audio speakers were low fidelity, rendering the soundtrack a garble that was beyond understanding. I found myself staring at the subtitles, hoping to wrangle some sense out of them. Hardly a perfect cinema experience, but there was something satisfying about it. Being there, watching the film, sharing the monastery hall with the work of an old heretic, life is made for such irony. Besides, it was a fund-raiser to purchase a projector for a village school up in the mountains. Kazantzakis, ever a partisan of the poor, would have been pleased.

> *Apostólyi owned the mountain above Apollona on the southern limit of the bay, which ended in a headland. He spent his life chasing a herd of goats and long-tailed sheep across the mountain at speed; we used to see him flying across the thistly scrub. He was part of the mountain, one saw this in his dancing. The Naxian dance employs exactly the steps as are used in treading the grapes, which is not extraordinary looking back on Dionysus' presence there. When Apostólyi performed this dance at the panygýri in summer he transformed it—using the sweeping movements of the eagle as it drops from a great height, the hissing sounds and coiling movements of a serpent, and the caprioles of the mountain goats, his daily companions.*
>
> Patience Gray, *Honey from a Weed*

Susan didn't like renting cars, preferring to mingle on buses and trains with regular folks, wherever we were. But she relented when we learned that the buses were out of season. Without a car, we couldn't get to Apollonas, a small town on the north coast of Naxos where Patience Gray and her husband lived for a year. When Susan read Gray's book on living off the grid and peasant cooking, she talked about it for days and the recipes populated the household menu. Nothing new, really. Susan had been cooking in a similar vein since I'd known her, preferring the foods closest to the earth. Patience Gray just added another handful of grist.

I tend to agree with Susan about car rentals. Driving in a foreign country offers little enticement; I might as well throw open the barn door of anxiety. However, I figured it might be worth putting up with that in order to see more of the island, which was far too big for pedestrian exploration. Susan suggested that we comparison shop for the best rental price. I groaned. We'd only been on Naxos for a day, but I'd noticed that there were more car rental agencies than any other single type of retail business, including restaurants. They languished in every nook and cranny, sometimes three to a block, jammed into tiny storefronts between cafes and boutiques. The usual brands, like Hertz and Avis, were subsumed in a carnival of local names like "Fun Cars," "Smile Naxos," "Tony's Bikes + Cars," "Naxos Vision," "Motoland," and, my favorite, "Apollo Rent A Car," implying that your conveyance would be a divine chariot. None of them contained actual cars, just the promise of cars, presumably stored elsewhere. It would take days to sift through this chaos. I'd prefer to pick one and be done with it. Having nothing else to fuss about in this paradise, we quarreled, and did nothing. At the end of the day, as we walked home, we passed a rental agency near our apartment. It was named "Naxosway" and its lights beamed out into the dark street. On impulse, we went in. A friendly middle-aged woman sat behind a desk at the back of the sparsely furnished office. We entered in a tentative state, still raw from the argument, but the woman's rosy smile chased away all doubt.

"Yes, yes, you can rent car." Her command of English was basic. She explained that if we wanted the only automatic transmission in the fleet, and we did, we would have to leave a deposit of ten euros. She bent over the desk to fill out a form in pen. There wasn't a computer in sight. "What is address?"

Sadly, we had no clue; we didn't even know the name of the street where we were staying. It was in Greek and the only time I saw a sign and deciphered it, I quickly forgot the name. We'd been delivered there straight from the ferry by Nikitas, our host along with Maria, his wife, so we never had to learn what it was called, we just knew how to walk through the streets to get there. We pointed vaguely and Susan fumbled to describe our location. "It's an apartment, Air BnB, just down the street..."

"Oh! Maria's studio?" She smiled again and we knew we were in the right place. Not only that, we were connected. The price quoted for the car was cheap, so we handed over a ten euro note and walked home in a good mood.

We showed up early in the morning, ready for our automotive adventure. The woman introduced us to a young man, perhaps her son since so many businesses in Greece are family concerns. He had more English, though less charm. We owed them twenty more euro and I offered my credit card.

"Cash is better," said the woman. Susan reminded me that the credit card provided car insurance, and I repeated that for the benefit of our agents. The two of them exchanged looks, then shrugged. "Cash is better," she reiterated, but she took the card anyway. Insurance didn't interest them, apparently, because they never mentioned it.

We gained further perspective when we walked outside with the man to get our car, parked in the middle of the street since there was nowhere else for it. This forced traffic to ease past through a narrow gap. We did a brisk walk around the car, noting various chips and dents. When we came to the passenger side, it was caved-in along the entire length. He dismissed it with a wave. "I did that myself." He sounded proud. "I forgot it was automatic transmission. Don't worry."

I couldn't figure out how the difference between an automatic and manual would result in crunching the side of the car, but since the doors worked and the vehicle looked new otherwise, I decided to take his advice and not worry about it. Eager to get on the road, we hopped in.

When we scheduled our outing, Susan expressed concern that the roads might be crowded on a Saturday. If true, at least we had a tiny car, like all the other cars trying to negotiate the narrow, winding roads of the Greek islands. Giant American automobiles look insane here, a true danger to self and others. After the harrowing bus ride on Crete, I was nervous about encountering drivers who like to play chicken, but as soon as we rolled out of Naxos Town, the roads were empty. For the entire day, we saw less than a dozen vehicles beyond the city. No wonder the buses shut down in the off season. Other than tourists, it's mostly farmers who use the roads. And goats, lots of goats. In some places the asphalt is littered with goat shit so dense as to resemble a plague of earthbound locusts.

The road curved along the coastal mountains, offering commanding views of the sea between the scattered hamlets. Everywhere we looked we saw raw marble. From the peaks to the shore, it was an island of marble. The quality of this stone lured Patience Gray's husband, "The Sculptor," just as it did the ancient Greeks. Builders started using Naxos marble almost three thousand years ago and the same stone is still mined and shipped around the world. The rock is so common here that the riprap shielding Naxos Town from the sea consists of giant marble blocks. The surface of the white stone glistens with large crystals of calcite, drawing the eye and the finger. On our first day, I picked up a sea-smooth lump on the beach and put it in my pocket as a souvenir.

Apollonas sits in a cove scooped out of the flanking mountain ridges, protected enough to support a few fishing boats that scurry to harbor when the wind blows from the north. On the hillside above the town is an old quarry, overgrown with stiff scrub. We parked the car in town and walked back up the hill on steep cobblestone passages, across the road and up the old trail to the quarry. It was famous for one thing: an incomplete *kouros* statue, thirty feet tall, still laying in the marble matrix after twenty-seven hundred years, rough shaped, waiting for transport to its destination where it could be finished. No one knows why it didn't get there. The leading conjecture sounds quite modern: they ran out of money.

Kouroi, as they are known in plural, were popular items in classical and pre-classical Greece. Life-size or larger replicas of slender, athletic young men, naked of course, they stand upright or as if on the verge of a step. Some say these statues are relics of the Apollo cult, examples of the god's fondness for young men, a predilection shared by many of his mortal followers. A polished *kouros* in Naxos marble would appear luminescent, like Apollo himself. No one knows how many were carved on the island and shipped to the mainland for installation in shrines, but over a hundred were installed in a single sanctuary near Thebes.

The town of Apollonas is named for Apollo, but the *kouros* in the quarry is a bearded, stockier figure. Dionysos, more like it. That's what the Naxians say, who have an affinity for Dionysos, the rescuer of their beloved Ariadne. Once a year, just before Lent, the islanders join in a Dionysian festival, men dressed as maenads, women as satyrs, frolicking, teasing, dancing, and making an unholy racket, just like the old ways. Perhaps they agree with Nietzsche that "...the Dionysiac element, as against the Apollonian, proves itself to be the eternal and original power of art...." For the Greeks, with their food, sensual aesthetics, and four-thousand-year-old culture, I thought that life itself was the great art, and the ferment of Dionysos its lubricant. Yet for all the deference given to the vine god, the sun of Apollo rides through the sky overhead, a constant radiance. It can't be ignored. You could be of both minds about this polarization. The chaotic landscape of Greek mythology yields endless contradictions. By some accounts, Orpheus wasn't an Apollonian at all, but a kind of secret agent for Dionysos. Regardless, it's not one or the other. As Nietzsche concluded, we need both.

After climbing on the massive, recumbent Dionysos and taking plenty of photographs, we scrambled around the rest of the quarry site, looking for other signs of the ancients while sacrificing bits of flesh and blood to the sharp thickets. We gave up quickly, choosing to perch on a slab of rock and gaze down the hill at the white-washed town, the sandy cove, and the sea beyond.

A German couple appeared out of the brush, escorting a scratched-up toddler. The man was convinced there were other gods lying around somewhere in the brambles and he was determined to find them. He clutched a map and some notes, which he waved with authority. We wished them good hunting but took it as a sign to walk away before getting sucked into their obsessions.

Back in the dented car, we drove south into the middle of the island to see the *kouroi* of Flerio, two more unfinished statues that didn't get far from the stone that gave them birth. We found a sign for the archaeological park at the entrance to an olive farm. Occupying a mountain glen, the farm covered hundreds of acres. Old, precise stone walls defined the complex of fields. In one place a large tree grew out of a six-foot retaining wall, its exposed roots integral to the rows of carefully laid stones. I puzzled over this. Trees pulled stonework apart, but this looked like a collaboration, perhaps a symbiosis of farmer and crop, adjusting the tree-nudged stones with a gentle hand, maintaining the interlocking mosaic of rubble and root over time.

Walking the paths through the farm put us in a dreamy state. Every step seemed to conjure a new idyll. A scrawled sign proclaiming "KOUROS" sent us up a narrow, wall-lined passage, dark under the shade of the arbors. As we reached the end of the passage and entered a circle of bare ground, I caught my breath and let the quiet fill me. Overhead the tree canopy formed an umbrella of olive and sycamore leaking dappled light. Stone benches projected from the wall around the periphery, inviting contemplation. I stepped slowly across the circle. Stretched out before me was the *kouros*, a ten-foot-tall man of rough marble, supine and relaxed, one knee slightly elevated. The undefined features suggested a universal being. One leg was broken, probably the reason it had been abandoned a few feet from the matrix where it was cut. I stroked the blank face of the *kouros,* a slender

Apollo. Yes, he slept, the kind of sleep that goes on for thousands of years.

Later, after we returned home, I read the following lines from Odysseus Elytis, the Nobel laureate from Crete:

And so many olive trees
  sifting the light through their hands
  so it spreads soft in your sleep

I read that passage over and over, thinking of the sleeping *kouros* and the languor that filled my bones as I stood over him.

We returned to the main trail and walked further, up another path, past the stone walls, past sheep tethered under olive trees, on up the hill and into the scrub that covers the uncultivated soil of the island. Eventually, we came to another clearing in the brush and the second *kouros*. Similar in posture and completion to the other, except the face had been sheared off and the legs broken at the shins. A few feet away, two carved marble boots stood side by side, as if waiting for the broken man to pull himself together, slip them on, and walk off.

I turned away from the fragments and lifted my eyes to absorb the view of the surrounding cliffs and mountains. I tried to haul it in, every beautiful bit, consuming it to feel it. Below, the olive trees cloaked the farm in shadows as the sun dropped to the west. What is it about a view that evokes a wholeness in the soul? I didn't know, I just savored it. We still had to return the car before dark, so we sauntered down the path into the trees. Deeply contented, I swung my arms and legs in freedom, feeling holy on the earth and in sync with the world.

Distracted with the wonder of life, I smacked headfirst into the pruned stub of a low-hanging olive branch. I moaned and staggered a few steps, hand to my throbbing forehead.

Susan picked up on it immediately. "What's wrong? What's wrong?"

About the time I had the sense to stop and breathe, I regained my speech. "I...I'm okay."

And I was, because for that one instant, clobbered by the olive tree, mind met matter and spirit and flesh were truly joined as one. A solid reminder that, no matter how lofty the aspirations, reality brings its own requirements, especially if you want to keep your body intact.

AFTERWORD

I owe a lot to my wife, Susan T. Landry. We wanted to tour ice age caves on our honeymoon in France, but she thought it would be foolish to wait for the wedding, so we went right away. It's been like that ever since. Spurred by her enthusiasm and meticulous planning, we've toured around Europe, following mutual whims, interests, and opportunities. We make a good team; even when we argue, we're both too interested in where we are to stay mad. Walking is the mainstay of our travel; it promotes flânerie and an educational pace. And public transport, though sometimes less convenient than a car, always provides a window into local culture. I'm pleased to have a travel companion who'd rather walk or take the bus; it's kept us in the flow of reality and peeled away some of the layers that insulate the tourist.

Along the way, we've met many people. Most of them have been helpful and kind. It's astonishing the amount of goodwill in the world, even when it seems like things are falling apart. I keep looking for the reflections of this goodwill in the politics of nations, but it's hard to find. Yet we've seen it and felt it within the interactions of daily life, and those experiences have helped to maintain what faith I have left. It would be impossible to acknowledge by name all these wonderful people, but without their assistance, our experiences would have been much poorer. No better example of such kindness can be found than Philippe Depallens, who provided us with astonishing, beautiful accommodations in Bonifacio, Corsica, drove us to trails, and took the photo that graces the author bio.

Then there are Nicole and David Ball, as stalwart friends as anyone could ask for. Not only did they let us stay in their Paris apartment for 8 months, but they encouraged us to return. If I ever had a question about French language, culture, or history, David provided prompt, comprehensive answers; our email correspondence must have a thousand entries by now. Most of these essays started out as letters to David (and sometimes Nicole), as I recounted our adventures for their amusement. Their friendship and generosity can't be overstated.

An essential component of our European journeys has always been meeting up with old friends Andreas Maurer and Rosa Quint in their beautiful, rustic dwelling in Liguria, Italy. They've fetched us from the train station time and again, fed us, lodged us, taken us to wonderful places, and best of all, they've shared the magnificent view from the olive terrace in front of their home, the best place in the world to watch the light fade from the sky.

My literary approach to traveling has never been consistent. I kept a journal sometimes, I took photos sometimes, I wrote emails, and posted tidbits on social media, but it amounts to little more than a tumbled heap of data. I read constantly in the literature of each locale, a pursuit that spawned quests to writers' former homes, museums, landmarks, streets, wherever things might be seen from a written perspective. Somehow, out of this hodge-podge of method and memory, a few stories of my own emerged.

BIBLIOGRAPHY

Bachelard, Gaston, *The Poetics of Space*, translated by Maria Jolas, Beacon Press, Boston 1969

Baudelaire, Charles, "Richard Wagner and *Tannhäuser* in Paris," *Selected Writings on Art and Literature*, translated by P.E. Charvet, Penguin Classics, London 2006

"The Seven Old Men," *The Flowers of Evil*, translated by James McGowan, Oxford University Press, Oxford 1998

Burkert, Walter, *Greek Religion*, translated by John Raffan, Harvard University Press, Cambridge, MA 1985

Debord, Guy, "Theory of the Dérive," *Situationist International Anthology, Revised and Expanded Edition*, edited and translated by Ken Knabb, Bureau of Public Secrets, Berkeley CA 2006

Deleuze, Gilles and **Felix Guattari**, *Anti-Oedipus: Capitalism and Schizophrenia*, translated by Robert Hurley, Mark Seem, and Helen R. Lane, Penguin Classics, New York 2009

Kafka: Toward a Minor Literature, translated by Dana Polan, University of Minnesota Press, Minneapolis 1986

Eco, Umberto, *Foucault's Pendulum*, translated by William Weaver, Harcourt, New York 2007

Elytis, Odysseus, *The Collected Poems*, translated by Jeffrey Carson and Nikos Sarris, Johns Hopkins University Press, Baltimore 1997

Gray, Patience, *Honey From A Weed*, Harper & Row, New York 1987

Haraway, Donna J., "A Cyborg Manifesto," *Manifestly Haraway*, University of Minnesota Press, Minneapolis 2016

Joyce, James, *Finnegans Wake*, Penguin Books, New York 1999

Kazantzakis, Nikos, *The Last Temptation of Christ*, translated by P.A. Bien, Simon & Schuster, New York 1998

Report to Greco, translated by P.A. Bien, Faber & Faber, London 1973

Knott, Eleanor, *Irish Classical Poetry*, Cultural Relations Committee of Ireland, Dublin 1960

O'Brien, Flann, *At Swim-Two-Birds*, Dalkey Archive Press, Normal, IL 2001

Sartre, Jean-Paul, *Being and Nothingness*, translated by Hazel Barnes, Washington Square Press, New York 1992

The War Diaries, translated by Quintin Hoare, Pantheon Books, New York 1985

James and Susan in
Bonifacio, Corsica
Photo by Philippe Depallens

The author lives with his dear wife in a creaky old house on the coast of Maine. He worked for thirty-five years as a psychotherapist specializing in family therapy and wilderness-based therapy. Before that he planted hundreds of thousands of trees in the industrial forest of the Pacific Northwest. During those years he lived off the grid, built log cabins, learned how to lay stone, and survived numerous exploits of mountaineering, rock climbing, and backcountry skiing. He is the author of several novels: *The Kraken Imaginary* (2022), *Rhizome* (2021) winner of the Maine Literary Award, *The Gorge of Despair* (2018), and a non-fiction work, *Mirror of Beasts: Episodes of a Reflected Ecology* (2013). Website: www.wrightjamesm.com

www.ingramcontent.com/pod-product-compliance
Lightning Source LLC
LaVergne TN
LVHW061047070526
838201LV00074B/5204